The Productivity & Decluttering Master Plan

Ninja Mind Hacks, Secrets & Habits To Become Productive & Organized, Stop Procrastinating, Save Time, Master Minimalism & Declutter Your Life, Home & Mind!

Russell Barlow

ALL COPYRIGHTS RESERVED.

Contents

CHAPTER 1 : AN INTRODUCTION TO THE
PRODUCTIVITY AND DECLUTTERING MASTER PLAN 1

CHAPTER 2 : HOW TO BE MORE PRODUCTIVE IN
EVERYTHING YOU DO 8

CHAPTER 3 : HOW TO DECLUTTER YOUR HOME,
LIFE, AND MIND 22

CHAPTER 4 : 10 TIME-SAVING SECRETS TO
EFFORTLESSLY BEAT PROCRASTINATION AND
BECOME MORE ORGANIZED 36

CHAPTER 5 : WHAT ARE THE LITTLE KNOWN
HABITS OF HIGHLY PRODUCTIVE PEOPLE? 45

CHAPTER 6 : THE SECRET HABITS AND NINJA MIND
HACKS TO BECOME THE MOST ORGANIZED PERSON
YOU KNOW 68

CHAPTER 7 : HOW TO MANAGE YOUR DAILY
ACTIONS TO BECOME MORE PRODUCTIVE AND
ACHIEVE MORE 86

CHAPTER 8 : HOW TO TRIPLE YOUR PRODUCTIVITY
OVERNIGHT WITH ONE SIMPLE STRATEGY 101

CHAPTER 9 : THE 3 SCIENTIFICALLY PROVEN THINGS YOU NEED TO STOP DOING RIGHT NOW IN ORDER TO GET MORE DONE.. 113

CHAPTER 10 : CONCLUSIONS WE CAN DRAW ABOUT IMPROVING PRODUCTIVITY AND DECLUTTERING OUR LIVES.. 135

Chapter 1

An Introduction to the Productivity and Decluttering Master Plan

One of the most daunting problems we face in the modern world is how to be more productive and how to declutter our lives. This book will study and recommend the most effective methods that we can utilize to achieve the changes we need. I will endeavor to explain techniques that will help you become more productive in a clear and concise manner.

Decluttering is something that most of us need to work on to become more productive. The modern trends in downsizing can demonstrate this. While we may not need to go so far as moving into a tiny home, the current reality is that we accumulate too much of practically everything. We all have room for improvement in our lives, and concentrating on decluttering is a positive step in becoming more productive.

Throughout the rest of this book, I will teach you everything you need to know to become the most productive person in your group. I will suggest strategies that will work both in business and on a personal level, which will lead to a more comfortable and more prosperous lifestyle.

Modern life is competitive; we all need to adjust and consider ways to get an edge on our competitors. Increasing productivity is an obvious way. Old habits can be hard to change, so we need to work on our mindset as we attempt to make positive changes in our lives. The power of positive thinking, as it were.

This guide will include plenty of detail that will help you affect dramatic changes in the way you approach things in your work and home life. Your aim should be to achieve the right balance of productivity in work and high quality of life.

We should have an active and productive day at work and still have time for a relaxing glass of wine and a great meal at the end of the day. None of us wants to work too hard, and there should always be plenty of time for family and friends. Increasing productivity at work is a great way to achieve this.

We need to learn methods which mean we can effectively use our time and effort to get what needs to get done - done! There is no single way to reach maximum efficiency; it is instead a matter of making incremental improvements over time.

We will study the methods used by highly productive people and see what we can learn from them. There are many ideas to consider, and we will decide on the best combination to put into effect.

They will be simple to implement, but effective.

I will suggest innovative tactics which will suggest things like Ninja mind hacks and secret habits to make your quest to become more productive more accessible. I will discuss how to be more productive in everything and anything you do and how to stop procrastinating and become a "doer."

Procrastination is the enemy of productivity and something that needs to be overcome to become efficient. There are various methods to discuss and then put into effect. There are certain habits of particularly productive people that we need to consider and analyze to see if we should implement them in our daily lives. There are some habits which we will consider dropping as they have been scientifically proven to hinder productive behavior.

Taking on too much work, a failure to say no, and not being decisive enough when it is time to delegate are perfect examples of this. Each issue does have an effective solution. I have run my own business for the past 15+ years, and it has become a personal quest to increase productivity both on a personal level and for my employees.

There are straightforward steps to be taken to improve team spirit and increase confidence. Sometimes it is as simple as some encouraging words, but even that can have a dramatic effect on productivity. Showing confidence in your team and encouraging them to learn new skills and take more responsibility are essential and practical steps to take.

Keeping up to date with technology and taking advantage of new hardware and apps is a constant theme with truly productive people. We will take a look at how best to follow their example. I will attempt to inspire you to achieve more with the benefit of my years of experience and hope to find the key to your productivity.

The fact is that we are all able to become more efficient and become more productive workers. All of this is applicable for both a billionaire business owner and a staff member with lesser responsibilities.

As I mentioned, there is no magic wand or one-step process. It is natural for us to take on new responsibilities as we gain more experience, so keeping our productivity high is an ongoing process. Time management is a skill we can all work on improving, and it is an evolving process. We will consider the latest methods which can help you become more productive.

I can offer you no "all solving" plan, or software, or a way to plan your which will solve all of your productivity issues. I can, however, offer you a series of methods which will have an overall effect. In a typical workday, there is much to do, whatever your responsibilities are. It is worth giving thought to how we can do more. Working harder is not always the best choice; working smarter is.

If you spend a little time the night before contemplating the day ahead and putting a list of goals to be achieved the next day along with a schedule together, you will increase productivity significantly. Whether it is motivating staff, selling products, building something great, merely answering your phone calls and emails or whatever it may be, we can all improve our efficiency.

Plainly stated, the more efficient we become, the more we get done. Productivity will lead to a higher income and a better lifestyle, so let's find the best solutions together! There are specific tools which I can recommend, which will make you more productive and provide you with tactics to effectively manage your time. There will also be tips on creating an environment in the workplace which stresses cooperation and teamwork to streamline operations.

Stress management is an essential factor to consider, and we will study this and recommend ways to keep your enthusiasm high and not risk burning out. Learning to relax, perhaps learning meditation and spending quality time with your loved ones and friends are all vital elements to remaining stress-free.

Positivity and realizing that all of us make mistakes is essential in understanding the appropriate steps to take to create efficiency. I aim to help you on a personal level and also to suggest techniques which will be useful in your business environment.

The way you plan your workspace is essential. It is vital that you feel comfortable. All of this will help you keep a clear mind, which will allow you to be more productive. Education is vital, and I would encourage you to help the younger members of your family to consider and learn these useful methods for leading a productive life.

Unfortunately, we usually do not learn to properly consider information, implement problem-solving skills, or develop efficiency during our schooling, but it is never too late! The majority of the methods I recommend here can also apply to your personal life, and it is often surprising how much extra time can be found to spend with family and friends by being more efficient.

If you try out and successfully learn the methods that I will teach you here, you will be well on the way to improving your productivity and getting more done.

Failure should never be considered the end. It should instead be a lesson and an opportunity to improve. The most successful business people have all faced setbacks and improved.

Exercise and diet are essential to consider concerning work; we should put together a healthy diet and a regular exercise program if we want to be at our most productive.

A great habit that most productive people often

share is getting up early in the morning. It allows them time to get more done when their competitors are asleep. Having this extra time can be the key to being more productive and for many people the saying "early to rise means healthy, wealthy and wise," is applicable. It can often help with mental clarity.

Many of us get too tied up in what is in front of us and fail to seek advice when we should. Highly productive people make a point of listening to others, and it is a desirable habit to pick up.

If at all possible, we should choose a business or job which we love to do. It will make doing the necessary hard work and being productive a pleasure. There are a limited amount of hours in a day, and we need to learn to make sure they all count! A successful life is not only judged on what we achieve in our work lives, but also in our relationships and the imprint we leave on the world.

Time management, finding innovative solutions, and keeping a smile on your face even during the toughest of times are all skills that we will consider together.

Join me in the following chapters, and we will look at all of the methods I have mentioned and learn how to put them all together to be the most productive person you can be.

Chapter 2

How to be More Productive in Everything You Do

There is little doubt that we can all find ways to improve our productivity. Perhaps the best approach is to make incremental steps in everything we do. Small steps lead to becoming more productive.

We all have multiple things to do to keep our lives running correctly. We have all experienced working hard, having to keep our family happy, and having a social life. The good news is humans are uniquely able to balance multiple responsibilities and even consider the best way to streamline what we do. We can function productively, even if it seems we are being overwhelmed with calls upon our time. The key is to keep a clear head, prioritize, and maintain a sense of humor.

All of this is an essential way of keeping in control of our lives and staying productive in a positive fashion. Common sense does go a long way when considering our best way to stay productive. We are all aware of how to efficiently use our time, but to stop feeling "snowed under" by life's responsibilities, we should consider the small changes that we could be making.

I will be looking at various methods to use these small changes to become more productive. These will be based on practicalities to help us improve. Most of us can do better and make our work, home, and social lives more productive. These seemingly insignificant changes can make a huge difference in our overall lives.

Many of us have choices to make about our work lives in regards to our decision-making process and ability to compartmentalize our work day. Old habits die hard. The simple process of "deciding to be more decisive" can have a significant effect on what we can achieve in one day at work. Maybe it is finally time to tell the office gossip that you are busy!

Prioritizing the levels of the importance we place on each task we need to fulfill into simple categories such as immediate, today, later, one day, etc. can be an effective way to improve productivity. It sounds simple; and it is, but we are all vulnerable to being indecisive and wasting precious time on something which does not need to be a priority.

Many highly productive people focus on clearing their minds and making use of time management techniques. We should learn from this. I will give various tips on how to manage your time at work, and many of these will apply to your personal life also. You can choose to use as many or as few of these as you wish, but I am confident that all of my methods will work for you to some degree.

The Workplace

A modern-day reality is that most of us feel we have too much work to do and not sufficient time to get it done. Perhaps we need to consider a few different tactics. It is essential to be realistic; if we take on considerably more than we have the resources to manage, we will get nowhere. There is little wrong with working hard, but we all have limits.

If we take on more than we can handle, our stress levels will rise. In my opinion, the key to productivity is to reach a balance. Do not be afraid to say no to extra work. Take on what you can realistically achieve, and don't be afraid to delegate whenever necessary. We all have limits on what we are capable of doing. The fact that we realize where our limits are is a big step to reaching maximum efficiency.

I am a big proponent of getting enough rest as it enables us to operate at an optimum level. "Early to bed, early to rise" is an expression most of us will remember from childhood, and it contains a lot of wisdom. We can learn from this.

You should make sure you like your surroundings in your workplace. We are all different, so identify where you feel most at ease. Being frustrated and feeling trapped is no way to live, so clarity and honesty with ourselves and others when it comes to what we hope to achieve is essential.

Training in the Workplace

Whichever level you work at, and whether you work for yourself or a huge, multinational company, it is crucial to keep up to date with the latest training. There is no doubt that the workplace is changing as technology develops at a tremendous rate. Old knowledge is outdated quickly. Whether it is signing up for a few online tech classes or taking advantage of your firm's latest training programs, it is vital to stay up to date.

The definition of the work we need to complete is no longer so clear. Many of us may feel that we could never finish it all to a satisfactory level, no matter how much time we have. All of this is where being realistic, deciding what is necessary, and prioritizing what we need to do comes in. Sometimes we must accept that not everything will be complete today. The fact that there is no easy definition of the work we do means we need to be decisive to find the best solution. We need to decide where the line for quality and content needs to be.

It is another reality that communication is becoming an increasingly important skill. Cross-department cooperation and discussion are necessary, and dealing with people is becoming an essential skill. Our jobs are changing, and very few of us spend time strictly working on what we were hired to do. The boundaries of what we will be expected to do are changing.

For example, a humble online writer ten years ago would have just been expected to provide the simple copy, but now Search Engine Optimization and providing links to reference sites are standard obligations. Keeping abreast of the latest innovations and training opportunities will enable us to become more efficient compared to our competitors.

So, we all need to be accepting that our responsibilities are increasingly flexible and consider how to equip ourselves best to deal with that. If we were able to assume our work description would stay the same, it would be far easier to master our work productivity. Unfortunately, this is a rare case these days. There are several reasons for this, and the main one is the trend to change jobs or the company we work for far more often than previous generations. A "job for life" rarely exists anymore.

Many of us work on flexible contracts and even for multiple employers at the same time, so it is understandable that different and evolving skills will become routine. Those of us at a later age, say in our forties or fifties, are more likely to change jobs than in the past, so there is a need to learn new technologies and business methods.

Many companies we work for or deal with are also likely to be more flexible in what they offer to clients, which will require more of us. A local food store is unlikely to supply food to only walk in clients anymore. They are likely to have a website and offer home delivery. So, the responsibility of an employee will change.

A manager of such a business, for example, would now have a much broader clientele to deal with and vastly more responsibilities, so learning new skills would be essential. Time management, responsible decision making, mastering e-commerce skills, and diplomacy with clients are all increasingly important.

Responsibilities seem to have blurred over the years; the best we can do is to stay adequately trained and keep up to date with business trends. There is a significant commitment we need to take to absorb the massive amount of information provided in the internet age. Daily, there seem to be new programs and apps to become familiar with and master. It hardly seems possible to be employable without access to the knowledge the internet provides us. We can assume that all of our competitors are up to date.

For instance, a new marketing campaign without considering social media advertising seems unlikely, but ten years ago, it would never have entered our heads. The internet has changed the world, and we need to adapt and change with it or be left behind in the dust. Technology is close to being able to replace us for many work functions with robots, so we need to stay competitive.

Old Work Habits are Obsolete

We can no longer rely on our education from school or college to get by in the modern work environment. Even a fresh graduate will be behind the times in a few months. In years gone by I remember people using a diary for appointments and considering it the height of being organized.

Then we went through a period of using online appointment setters or devices such as Palm Digital Assistants (PDA's), and the reality is today's business world is more sophisticated. We each seem to have a smartphone, tablet device, or laptop permanently attached to the end of our arm, so appointments or communication can be organized immediately. We need something more adaptable and able to assist us with the speed and adaptability required to be a productive member of the modern workforce. The ways we used to use to manage our time are no longer sufficient. We need to ensure we keep up with modern technology.

There are new methods used, and the day when a simple "to do" list was sufficient will not be seen again. The new reality is we may be dealing with 100's of work-related emails per day, and all of them seem to need an answer or an action immediately. We need to be disciplined and not let this take over. It is essential to set aside a certain period each day to handle work-related emails, or we risk losing track of other vital jobs. For sure, we need useful tools to assist us, but we also need a new way of thinking. It is vital to make immediate decisions and become more efficient.

Business Gurus and Training

It seems impossible to go online without being confronted by some new business advisor promising riches if you follow him or buy his course. I have reviewed many of these business training courses or money-making opportunities, and all I will say is consider all sides when choosing them. That is not to say there is not honest advice from good people out there, but for the majority of these courses, it is purely a money-making venture from which you will gain little.

There comes the point when you have to question why there are so many "Gurus" out there who have the perfect secret to wealth and productivity? Surely, if they were that talented and wise, they would be using their skills to make their own money in business. The sad fact is, most of them don't have much business ability, but they are good at persuading you to pay for their training course and then sell it on their behalf through affiliate marketing.

A lot of this is designed to use you to make them ever-increasing profits. There is a more excellent and lucrative use of your time. They typically encourage thinking of "the big picture," which is not always a good thing. Getting the necessary day-to-day things right is still a key element in business success. While we may think that identifying our values and clarifying goals will help us become better organized and efficient, there is often too much going on in day-to-day business to focus on that.

In my opinion, you need to have as much information as possible, and then you will be your own best guru. The bigger picture will not help you when you have 100 emails to answer. Focusing on "the big picture" is essential, but it will not be much help in our quest to become more productive. If anything, it will confuse the issue and slow us down.

We Need to be in Control to be Productive

If we think back to times when we can honestly say we were at our most productive, it is almost certainly a time that we felt in control of what we were doing. If you are stressed out or worrying about an issue with your boss or staff, you will be likely to overreact to things and achieve less and be ineffective.

We need to find a level of calmness and relaxation to be genuinely useful. There are many ways that we can achieve this, and you will need to find out what works best for you. For some, it might be meditation or simply calmly reflecting on your day. Others may achieve this through a quiet meal with their partners; and others through an evening of drinking with colleagues. The point is to find a way that enables you to have the mindset that you are in control. All of this added to a clear mind will allow us to operate at an improved productivity level.

The trick is, when you feel out of control, overwhelmed, bored, what do you do to get your feeling of control back? Later in this guide, I will run through strategies which have worked for me in the past, and it will be for you to adapt them and discover what works best for you. We are all able to improve.

How to Deal With Yourself

One of the main challenges we face in improving our productivity is how to maintain focus and have the right mindset. We tend to make promises and deals with ourselves, which affect the way we think and impact a positive mindset. We need to change this and find a better way of dealing with things that are on our mind. It seems that the human mind is predisposed to complicate things for itself. We need to think of methods to overcome this and reach a state of clarity.

We can commit with ourselves to do practically anything. It could be large or small. It could be to fire your assistant or to buy a subtler brand of coffee for the office. Whatever these deals with yourself are, it is crucial to act on them right away. If you let them fester, you will be distracted and lose efficiency. You are likely to have made more of these deals with yourself than you realize, and each one will be on your mind at some level. They will be dragging your attention away from where it needs to be. You have to be decisive and handle all of these internal commitments so that you can move on.

There are methods to achieve this. There should be a pledge to recognize and list these deals you make with yourself and keep working through them until they are all solved. If they are playing on your mind, you will never have clarity and be able to perform at your most productive level. A practical method to deal with this is to decide what major deal you have made with yourself, and then work your way down the list. It could start with something significant and run to something seemingly insignificant. The critical part will be to decide to solve each one. In fact, write it down to remind yourself.

These will enable you to feel that you have taken some practical action to overcome these issues and give you a feeling of having found some control. This is important for your mindset. Just running these issues through your thought process and committing to do something about them will be enough to help you become more productive. If you are mindful of problems, you can improve them.

We can Train Ourselves to be More Productive.

It is possible to train ourselves like a martial artist or a boxer does, to be more responsive, quicker thinking, and faster overall. While training the body, and being in good condition is an advantage for most of us, the training here is mental. Having clarity of mind is essential if we wish to be productive. We can learn to think more efficiently and either resolve or tune out distractions in either our work or personal lives. The mind is a stunningly powerful tool, and it can be taught to be disciplined.

The aim is to achieve more by using less time-consuming effort. You can make rules to overcome unnecessary distractions and find a solution to being overburdened in all aspects of our lives. You need to keep a clear mind; and one effective way to achieve that is to manage what you do. There are only a certain number of actions you can undertake in one day. You need to make them count.

You need to consider what you will achieve in a day, with your work, with your personal life, and with your mind. Find a way to manage your actions. You must clarify what actions will allow you to move forward. You may have a work project which seems impossible, but finding the right step to take will solve it. Being organized and aware of the issues you face and having a desire to solve them are a big part of becoming more efficient and productive. Learning to identify issues at the beginning of a project and not leaving then until it is too late is an important skill to utilize. Take action at the beginning!

Clearing Your Mind is Key

To reach the feeling of being in control, you need to find your optimum state of mind. In my opinion, the best way to do that is to clear your mind thoroughly. There is no way to be efficient with a cluttered mind. I always try to empty my mind to be able to focus on tasks at hand. You need to leave your troubles and concerns behind you and focus on what is essential right now. There are always issues to deal with, so I recommend you separate them from your mind and use whatever tools you have at your disposal.

You can list the things that bother you then find an appropriate action. You can delegate; you can find an immediate solution; or you can decide it doesn't matter, just so long as you deal with it. It is essential not to be distracted by incomplete thoughts. All too often, we overburden our minds with tasks or questions we can either solve or disregard.

Many of us find that our minds wander when we should be focusing on a task at hand. It is due to something unresolved preying on our minds. How can we be efficient if that is occurring? All of this can cause stress and limits the amount of time we have to dedicate to anything we wish to achieve.

Too many people have a constant state of stress because they have too many things on their minds, which means they can't be productive, which in turn means there is not enough time. It is all interrelated, and without making demonstrable changes, we will never find a way to improve our efficiency and be at our most productive. We need to find ways to relieve ourselves of this stress.

We usually underestimate how much pressure we are under and only notice when we feel better after solving the underlying problem. This is why we feel like celebrating after finally completing a long and challenging project. It is a similar case here; solve the issues you face, and you will feel in control of your life. In short, we need to free our minds to feel in control, and this will enable us to work efficiently and operate at a maximum level of productivity.

Chapter 3

How to Declutter Your Home, Life, and Mind

One crucial way to boost our productivity is to declutter our lives. This means in all forms - our homes, our lives in general, and our minds.

Let's first consider our home. There are practical reasons why we need to declutter it. We can then live a more ordered and less distracted life. Recent years have seen a trend for people downsizing in their personal lives. The trend toward tiny houses is inspiring. It proves that many of our possessions are not needed to be happy. We really should analyze just how much "stuff" we need to keep. Does the football shirt leftover from college need to be saved? There is an excellent argument to be made that having fewer possessions, means we have less to worry about - so we will be better off.

Decluttering Your Home

There are different reasons why we allow our home to get cluttered and disorganized. It could be the stresses of everyday life, laziness, or something more complex.

Taking care of a family, working hard, and an active social life could all play a part. Often a new baby, or even pet dog, can disrupt things and lead to a cluttered environment. Any changes in circumstance, perhaps a new job or being away from home for a training course, can cause us to lose control of our ordered lives. We need to identify and correct this.

Once things get out of control, a lot of us subconsciously give up and accept the clutter building up around us. It is a symptom of a stressed mind and will adversely affect our productivity levels. The question is, what can we do about it? To be productive, we need to have organized surroundings. A clean and decluttered house is a necessary part of having a clear mind. We can't expect to be living in chaos and to be at our best. We have to stop being disorganized, stop putting things off, and make some decisions. It is time to make some changes!

Whatever your path to clutter has been, you need to make a conscious decision to make a change. Analyze why it has happened and identify what to do about it. The following section of this guide will make recommendations; and you can use it to help make positive changes to your surroundings. We need to get rid of the chaos and find some order.

Does my Home Have an Issue with Clutter?

You would think that it would be easy to tell if you have too much clutter; but sometimes our familiarity with our surroundings means we don't notice it building up until it is overwhelming. The signs are when you start to notice there are papers everywhere. Perhaps there is too much dirty washing or kids' toys.

This can get increasingly worse until you start to find newspapers from a few years ago and to have difficulty finding a place to sit down. It is easy for our minds to find excuses when this happens. You may have trouble finding things that you look for and end up buying things you already have. Does this sound like a person in control? Try to improve your awareness of this. It should bother you.

Before we know it, we get used to this state of calamity, and it becomes the new normal. It can start to feel like there is no way of changing it. Living like this means you are making things unnecessarily difficult for yourself, and there is undoubtedly a better way. You cannot be at your best in such a complex environment. The good news is you can easily decide to do something about it and create something new and improved!

How to Make a Change

Firstly, learn to notice the signs that the clutter in your home is getting out of control. Is the washing up always piled up in the sink and you only ever think of washing it when there are no more plates available to use? Is your bed in a permanently messy state? Is this due to your subconscious saying to you, what's the point of making your bed; you will be sleeping in it again in a few hours? Just how long has it been since you properly ironed your clothes? Or hung them up in the wardrobe properly?

Do you have unopened mail and you read newspapers and magazines from years ago, just because they are close to hand? Is your garage so full of junk that your car has been parked out in the street for months? Are you afraid to let your family and friends see the state of it? Are the kids' toys everywhere, and are they following your approach to leaving things lying around? Lead by example, not by sloppiness!

Do you have many, different half-used soaps and other toiletries in your bathroom? Are the cupboards full of things you will never use? Is everything so cluttered that you are starting to have trouble finding your car keys in the morning?

If all, or even some of, these questions are an issue in your house, it is time to make a positive change. You are living chaotically, and there is no way your mind is at its most productive.

Firstly, recognize that there is a problem and decide to make a change. Write it down and leave it somewhere you will always see it. Keep a list of all of the inconveniences that the state of your house causes. These could include having to wash plates when hungry or never having an ironed outfit ready in the morning. Keeping a record of all of this will emphasize to you that there is a problem and it will serve to keep you determined to do something about it. There is a better and more ordered way of living!

Put a System in Place to Start Decluttering

One step at a time is the key here. You have already made a good start by writing down the inconveniences the state of your home is causing you, and your determination to make positive changes.

Don't be overwhelmed by the task at hand and get into negative thought patterns such as "I will never fix this. It is pointless to try." Also, don't be tempted to do a quick fix by putting all of your junk into a cupboard and pretending it has gone away. This situation needs a proper solution! There is no point by trying to fool yourself.

Don't try to do everything at once and make a start all over the house. Discipline and planning are necessary to regain control. Develop a plan to tackle each part of your home in stages. Why not make a start in the kitchen? A clean area to prepare food and have all of the plates and cutlery in the right place will feel like a positive step. Breaking the project into parts will make it feel like a more straightforward process and encourage you to keep going.

Visualize the result and think of a well-organized, clean, clutter-free home and how good that will feel. It is an essential step to regaining the feeling that you are in control. The fact is you have adapted to your old careless ways, and it has become the norm. You need to retrain your brain and pledge to yourself that once this is solved, you will not go back to your old ways.

Some houses you visit may seem well-kept, clean, and orderly on the surface, but have drawers and cupboards full of junk when you look deeper. Don't let that that be your future! This is a trap to avoid, as we are not interested in appearances, but having a truly decluttered environment. Having something beautiful to show people is not enough. The fact that you tidied up and did a bit of vacuuming is missing the point I am trying to make here. You need to make a real change rather than a cosmetic one.

When you finally do get organized, you should aim to have a purpose for every cabinet and drawer, and not just use it as a storage place for unnecessary junk. Mindfulness is a part of having a clean home. We should plan everything in an organized way. All of this may seem inconsequential, but it is a factor in becoming more efficient. Our mental clarity is vital to our productivity and the environment we live in today. A disorganized and chaotic place will affect you in myriad ways.

The next time you come home, imagine that it is someone else's place. What is your impression of it? Have a look around; open some drawers. Does it seem like an organized place? Is it a real mess? Are some areas, like the kitchen or garage particularly chaotic? What is your overall impression? If it is negative, there is an issue which will need to be worked out. Giving yourself some distance and looking at the state of your home as if you were an outsider is an effective way to start planning for getting organized. All of this may also help you realize that things are not as bad as you had feared and make starting the decluttering process seem possible and realistic.

You need to get a system in place. Establish the main problem areas of your home and make a start. One room first; and commit to getting the task complete within a fixed schedule. Another right way ahead is to develop some day-to-day practices and stick to them. You can try to clean the kitchen every day, including all plates and cutlery. Throw out all of the garbage each evening and make the bed each morning after you get up. Simple things matter!

Make a list of ten things like this to do each day and write them down and make them a habit. Include something unconventional, like brushing your teeth with your other hand. This will act as a reminder to do the less pleasant tasks, and all of this is a useful mental process to start making a change. Subconsciously, you are already becoming more efficient and productive. You can and will find the best system that works for you to declutter your home. And it will feel like a weight off your mind when you do.

Remember that we all can get organized. A written list of new habits to follow will be a big help; and dividing the steps to take will make that process easier. All of these steps we have discussed help us regain control over our environment and get us in a more productive state of mind.

Decluttering Your Home Office is a Way to Improve Your Productivity at Work.

It is a new reality that most of us do at least some of our work at home. Whether that means telecommuting or merely responding to a few emails in the evening, a nicely organized home office is vital. Nobody will work efficiently in a chaotic environment, so leaving the dirty plates from last week's midnight snack and a pile of dirty clothes next to the computer will never be a good thing.

An excellent place to start will be to do a quick fix. Take a few hours to throw out anything unnecessary and give the room a good clean. You should take this opportunity to make a promise to yourself to never let clutter take over again and organize your home office every morning. Write it down and leave it somewhere visible. By managing the clutter and cleaning up every day, it will only take a matter of minutes. You will never have to face hours of throwing out the junk in this room again.

An orderly home office will help give you a

feeling of control, which, as we have discussed, is vital to having a clear mind and becoming more efficient and productive. The next step should be considering the best way to organize your desk. Is there something we can do without or something that we should add? We should only have things in our home office that we need and serve a useful function. Consider your setup and the best way to refine it.

Let's look at a few useful points to consider and create a plan to set up an efficient and effective home office. What exactly will space be used for, and are all of your tools up to date? Perhaps it is now time to upgrade your laptop and invest in some new hardware.

Is your workstation and chair a comfortable fit for you? Do you have enough cabinets for your files, and is there an area to store old documents? All of this may sound simple; but it is crucial. Think of small, practical steps to make your life easier while working at home. Make sure your filing system is within easy reach of your desk, and that reference books are close to hand. Make sure there is adequate shelving to stop the build-up of clutter. Invest in some more bookcases if you need more storage space.

Lighting is essential for most people. It affects our mood, and being too dark or too bright is not advisable, so it is worth investing in some good, adjustable overhead lights and lamps. You need to define what the room is for. Is it strictly your workspace, or can your kids use it for doing their homework? If there are other uses sometimes, like watching TV, give each activity its own space.

These are all simple methods that will make working in your home office a happier experience and help you become more productive.

Effective Methods to Declutter our Life and Mind

Decluttering your home is a good start, but we need to consider the best ways to do something similar with our life and mind. Earlier on, we have discussed that achieving a clear mind and taking out unnecessary distractions is the way to become more productive.

The fact is, many people have a cluttered mind, which in many ways is worse than a cluttered home or workspace. There are a few straightforward ways we can declutter and reach the clarity we need. Too much clutter in our mind will make us restless and make it difficult to focus. It will cause us to be distracted and make it difficult to get things done. Promise yourself that you will change it.

Some things that we can refer to as "Clutter of the mind" are overthinking things, going over past experiences, again and again, having worries about the future and feeling overburdened. In a way, our mind is a little bit like a hard drive on a computer, and there are ways to delete unnecessary clutter and create some space. Give it a regular checkup in our mind.

Let's consider some ways to declutter our mind so that we can have more clarity and achieve more. We have already discussed ways to declutter our physical space at home and work. It is essential to sort this out as excessive stimuli will impede our ability to be productive. We can declutter our lives in other ways. Perhaps we can look at our social lives, and maybe we can miss the occasional drinking session with friends or game of golf.

Write down the steps you decide to take, either in a journal or download an app. All of this helps to store information outside of the mind and free up some space. We can add appointments, ideas, etc. Keeping a general journal is an excellent way to expand on the previous point, and a way to keep track of our thoughts. It will allow us to note down our concerns, which act as a distraction to getting things done - and ultimately, being productive.

You can keep a written record of the following:

- Goals which are essential to you, and how to achieve them.

- Things which affect your confidence and energy, such as worries about a relationship

- General things which prey on your mind and worry you.

- Everyday tasks that will help your life stay more ordered.

Keeping a journal is also an effective way to discipline our minds, by taking a set period per day to write and reflect on what our day was about and what needs to be focused on tomorrow.

You should let go of the past. Let it go and don't let it bother you. Whatever has happened, put it down to experience and think of the positive. Plans for revenge or changing the past don't work out well.

Multi-tasking is not always practical. There is a time and also a place for everything. Devote a set period of time to each task. Let your mind be free and ignore distractions that come into your mind. Choose to be more decisive. Most of us feel overburdened at work and often with our home lives. We need to decide what is most important and deal with those issues one by one.

Many of us suffer from receiving too much information, whether it is from newspapers, surfing the internet, social media, or watching too much TV. Again, this will lead to a lack of clear thinking. To avoid being preoccupied with all of his information, we should limit what we take in. We should set a time limit on our time spent online and choose the content we follow carefully. Make a conscious effort only to read or watch things which are of benefit to you. Try to cut out the nonsense and only take in relevant information and ignore the rest.

We should be more decisive. In the same way that we should decide what to do with the 100's of emails we receive, we need to do similar with the information our brains, or it will be overcrowded. A cluttered mind will not function properly. Your decision-making process is essential. And don't procrastinate. Decide what to do with the information you have. Either disregard it or take action on it.

The small things in life can take up too much time and energy. For mundane tasks such as breakfast, what to wear, and what to take to work for lunch, make a policy and stick to it. There is no need to spend time each day considering the small things over and over. Get into a routine and get the little everyday things off your mind by doing them automatically.

Meditation may be a useful practice to help clear and discipline the mind, whether it is a formal process such as a Buddhist may use or only taking some time to do some deep reflection. Basically, meditating will allow you to focus on one thing at a time - for example, breathing - and clear your mind. One thing at a time is always a good policy to adopt. It is almost like taking your mind to the dry cleaners and getting all of the wasteful clutter washed away. Most of us need this. Meditation is undoubtedly an effective way to get rid of unnecessary thoughts, regain focus, and have a balanced feeling which will help us become more productive.

We need to learn to prioritize every part of our lives to feel happy and have a clear mind. An endless list of things to do will clutter the brain and lead to being unproductive. We should know what our top priorities are and focus most of our brain power on doing those things. There is no point having an endless to-do list running through our minds.

We have seen there are various ways to declutter multiple parts of our lives. We need to choose which are the most applicable to us and decide on the best methods to deal with it. Clutter in our minds leads to a build-up of random thoughts and information in our inside worlds. It stops us being able to think clearly and affects our ability to focus on what is essential.

Decluttering our mind is one of the most powerful things we can do if we wish to be more focused. Seriously consider working on this. Following the methods mentioned above will be an ideal way to declutter your life and will enable you to feel mentally clear. Declutter your home, life, and mind, and you will be well on the way to achieving an optimum level of productivity in your life. You will notice improvements at work and in your life at home.

Chapter 4

10 Time-Saving Secrets to Effortlessly Beat Procrastination and Become More Organized

Procrastination is something even the most disciplined and effective amongst us will face from time to time. It is the enemy of productivity. For some of us, being under pressure as we have left things to the last minute is a worrying thing to dread and will lead to panic and a substandard quality in our work. For others of us, overthinking things and leaving everything until the deadline is almost here is a way of life and a situation to thrive. We are all different and work best under different conditions.

However, for many of us, procrastinating will make our home and work lives suffer. And when that starts to occur, it is time to decide to do something positive about it.

I will now run through a few proven methods to help you with your time management, reduce procrastinating to get more done, and reduce the need to racing against the clock.

Fix a Deadline, and Then Follow it.

One of the best ways to overcome an issue with procrastinating is to set a fixed deadline and commit to it by letting other people know about it. For example, you may need to complete a sales report and not feel into doing it. However, if you tell everyone there is a meeting to discuss it on Monday morning, you won't have time to procrastinate.

It is human nature not to want to let people down and have to rearrange everything, so you will find your mind keen to get on with it. Even if this is a self-imposed deadline, you can treat it as if your boss created it and honor it in the same way. Nobody wants to let the boss down, and your mind indeed won't.

This method works well for me, especially if there is something that needs to get done, and I am struggling to get motivated. Make an appointment to discuss your project and follow it.

Start With a Small Step

We all suffer from times when we don't feel motivated, or when we don't fancy doing what we need to get done. Let's imagine it is a report which needs to be complete by the weekend and you can't seem to get motivated. Something which always helps me in this situation is to take a small step. It may be as simple as noting down the headlines and titles. It will get your subconscious mind thinking about the subject. You may have then given it more thought than you have realized.

I often try to do his last thing at night if I know I have to write the next day. More often than not, I end up making a decent start and getting quite a lot done. All of this will make a massive difference in your mindset. Even the smallest step means you have made a start and makes the overall process seem more achievable.

It will have the effect of disciplining your mind to get used to the activity each day, and you will get used to the idea that it is not so bad. Hopefully, the endorphins will kick in, and soon you will be enjoying the process, and an hour per day will start to fly past. Taking even the smallest steps toward your goal is always a good start, and it will help you fix any issues you may have with getting motivated.

Just taking a step will allow you to overcome any mental block you may have, stop procrastinating, and become better organized.

Put up a Do Not Disturb Sign

Issues with procrastinating can often stop by exercising self-discipline. Lock yourself away, let everyone know not to disturb you, turn off your phone, and set a time for your project's deadline. You need to write down your intentions, when it needs to be complete by, and turn off any distractions which will tempt you to get sidetracked.

If you regularly do this, it will start to be like muscle memory. So, set the scene to do what needs to be done and create the environment to be able to focus efficiently. It is a beautiful way to increase your discipline, overcome procrastination, and become a more organized person. Give it a try and see for yourself.

Don't be so Hard on Yourself.

Many of us tend to feel bad about procrastinating and our lack of ability to get motivated to get things done. We should, too. It impedes our ability to be productive. However, we should understand that we are human and stop being so hard on ourselves. We are not bad-intentioned, not all wrong; we are just human beings.

Instead, we should focus on the positive and concentrate on just getting a little more done each time and getting closer to our objective. Overcoming Procrastination and becoming more organized can be a gradual process, and a step by step approach is realistic.

Accentuate the Positive

It would be best if you always considered the positive outcome and reward that will come with it when you are contemplating doing something.

Whether it is picking up your son's bike from the repair shop or making a phone call to complete a sale for work, most things come with a reward. In these cases, a happy child or boss. It is an effective way for you to overcome a tendency to procrastinate and focus on a positive outcome. The reward is usually worth the effort.

Most of us feel happy after achieving something, and there is often a satisfaction in that, no matter how small it may seem. Motivation comes in many different forms.

We Need to Understand Why We Procrastinate

There is no need to go so far to pay for therapy, but doing some amateur scientific or detecting work is useful to help us understand why we face issues with procrastinating and getting organized. We can start by noting down our thoughts, moods, and patterns of behavior when we feel we are procrastinating.

Some of us may be perfectionists, whether we realize it or not, and the need to get things right can cause us doubts, which lead us to delay things. If we can better understand our pattern of behaviors, we can reduce our doubts and anxieties about this and gain positive thoughts about doing what we set out to achieve.

Understanding ourselves and why we do things will lead to more exceptional organization and increased productivity. The key is being objective when we consider why we do the things we do.

Reward Yourself When You Complete a Necessary Task

One effective way to help overcome procrastination is to write a list of things that need to be done and separate them into things you feel happy to do and those that you can't get motivated to start. Please start with the least appealing task and assign yourself a reward for when you complete it. It could be something simple like a chocolate bar, a nice glass of wine, or an hour of your favorite TV show.

Next, do one of the more delightful tasks, and after that, alternate. It will make it mentally more natural to work through all of the functions. The brain does enjoy getting rewarded and will respond to this method.

It is an excellent way to get more organized and start to achieve more. If increased productivity is the ultimate aim, little tricks like this that we can play on ourselves are an effective way to make it.

Discuss Your Schedule with a Partner

Choosing a partner, possibly a work colleague, whom you will feel accountable to, is an excellent way to overcome procrastination issues. It can work in favor of you both as you can both encourage each other and feel responsible for your partner to get things done on time.

The mind is a strange thing. And it hates to let other people down, so making that commitment can be a truly effective way to get properly organized. It can be employed in other parts of our lives aside from the workplace as well. If you commit to saying you will lose weight by going jogging every day and discuss it with a partner, it will help with motivation. You will avoid thinking about getting up and going for a run in the morning if you have made a commitment and promised your partner. No more procrastinating!

Many of us know we need to achieve something and we keep delaying it as we do not commit to following it for anybody else. It is always too easy to make excuses for ourselves. Discuss the schedule with a partner and get their help to help make you follow it and make it clear that you will do the same for them.

It is essential to have the right partner whom you will feel accountable to, and he or she will be able to assist you to overcome procrastination and become more productive.

Have Some Set Daily Tasks

There will always be times when you will not feel like doing something. An excellent way to overcome this is to set some failsafe daily tasks, a few things that you commit to doing, no matter what happens or how you feel; something that you can't negotiate about with yourself.

It could be anything which is strictly necessary. For example, it could be a report on the sales achieved by your team and an update of their expense reports while on the road. If you commit to completing both of these tasks at the end of each day, it will become a habit that you will not break as you have already made a firm commitment to yourself. It will become second nature and something you will never need to procrastinate. It will lead to an improvement in your work practices.

Have a Separate Time for Procrastination

There is nothing to stop you from setting aside a period per day to sit and procrastinate about things. However, you should schedule it, and stick to it. Some of us quite enjoy the process of procrastinating. So, if that is the case, we could use it as a set period per day as some others use for meditation. Ideally, you can schedule this during a period that you will not be working. It could be while you are washing the plates or waiting for your child's soccer practice to finish.

It would be best if you tried to be disciplined about it and set a set period every day so that it does not interfere with your work time. Marking this time in your schedule may eliminate many of the adverse effects associated with procrastinating and allow you to have a clear and refreshed mind when you start to do your daily tasks.

To conclude, overcoming procrastination is best

done by using disciplines and methods like these. It would be best if you committed to do or change things and stick to it. Use these ten methods to become more organized and stop letting procrastinating being such a negative in your life.

Being more productive is an aim that we should all strive for, and it is entirely possible if we implement a new way of doing things and a new mindset.

Chapter 5

What are the Little Known Habits of Highly Productive People?

There is a lot to be learned from the habits of others, and I would like to take a look at some of the practices adopted by highly productive people. There is a lot to be learned from people who are elite in their field, whether it is business, sports, or the arts. They seem to have a thirst for success and endless energy and spirit. How do they achieve it?

The first thing that becomes apparent is that we should aim to work smarter rather than working for all hours under the sun. Increasing our efficiency is a way to increase productivity.

Let's look at some examples:

You Need to Eliminate Distractions

It is a golden rule for particularly productive individuals. They recognize that this will slow them down, and they will seek out ways to minimize the issue.

I used to have a cleaner in my office, who was unbelievably chatty. The staff member was a nice woman whom I didn't wish to offend, but every time I saw her, she would take up fifteen minutes of my time. Although it was a hard thing to do, I decided I needed to explain that I was busy, and I only had time to chat after work. I blamed it all on my boss!

If your workspace is too loud and you find it a distraction, buy yourself a good headset and put some inspiring music on your phone to listen to while you work. Don't open websites on your computer that are not relevant to the task at hand. There is time to read about sport at home later! By being aware of the distractions you face and making the decision to minimize them, you will increase the amount of work you get done dramatically and become a far more efficient worker.

Similarly, in your home life, forgoing an extra glass of wine in the evening may allow you to get your house cleaned without distraction. You can always have it as a reward later. A minimal amount of disciplining ourselves concerning stopping distractions will lead to greater efficiency and lead to us becoming more productive. It is worth the effort.

Multitasking Will Slow You Down

People who practice multitasking may think that they are achieving a lot, but it is a proven way to be less effective. It slows down our mental process and makes us less efficient. Going from job to job is not an effective way of working. Concentrating on one task over an extended period is the best way to get things done. It allows for deep concentration and effective results.

Imagine a rock star struggling with writing a new album. He is likely to be better off focusing on finishing the song at hand than jumping from one to the other. Discipline and being determined to finish what is in front of us is the best way to be productive. Multitasking is the enemy in his instance.

Practice eliminating multitasking at work and during your home life, and you will notice an improvement in your productivity. Do it today, and don't procrastinate!

Don't Always Focus on Your Emails.

Receiving 100's of emails every day seems to be a current reality. You would be amazed at how much time per day you can lose by leaving your inbox open. It is human nature to want to deal with things as we become aware of them, so genuinely productive people limit the times that they read their inbox.

It varies from person to person, but I like to spend an hour when I first arrive at my work desk, an hour after lunch, and an hour at the end of the day contemplating and answering emails. Being selective of when I deal with it means I get far more done. It just takes a bit of discipline.

If you have someone (perhaps your boss or an important client) that needs to be dealt with urgently, you can always set up an alternative email which will alert you, but overall spend time on other work. It is a particularly effective method used by productive people, and you should try to implement it into your work day. It will make a big difference.

Similarly, it would be best if you disciplined yourself at home to not be a slave to answering emails. Your family deserves quality time with you, so fix a time to check any critical emails. A half hour at night is perhaps the best way to do this. Then you can sleep with the knowledge that you can start the next day with everything up to date.

Taking Small Steps is Key

Highly efficient people will always approach a large project by making it seem more achievable by dividing it up. A massive job may seem overwhelming and make it seem challenging to start. If you make a start and go step by step, you will make good progress.

Make a list of achievable steps to take, and the project will start to feel more manageable. It will motivate you to keep going and know that you are making progress. It would be best if you overcame the feeling that the job is too much to handle and resist the temptation to procrastinate. If I am working on a book project, I like to start with an accessible introduction and then choose a chapter which I am most familiar with the subject and work on that.

We all have our methods to enable us to complete large projects, but making a start and working through it step by step is always a good practice to have. Psychologically, seeing the actual process will naturally inspire us to keep going and make completing a task seem possible. Step by step is an excellent method to help yourself stay motivated.

Implementing this method into our work day will help us become more efficient and get our projects completed more quickly. Try it and see.

Don't be Afraid to Make Mistakes.

The most productive people don't have a fear of failure. When things go wrong, it is the time to use it as an experience to learn from and to encourage us to improve.

There is no need to over-think what has gone wrong. The best course of action is to redouble your efforts and get productive again. There is nothing to gain by being inactive and worrying about making another mistake. People are human, and we need to realize that mistakes happen to the best of us. Don't get down about it.

If you wish to become truly productive in the jobs you do, you should embrace the element of risk. It is an essential way to develop your skills. Accept it as a part of what you are doing. Many successful and wealthy business people have experienced failure and gone broke at some point. Their ability to keep going and improve is what makes them a success.

We should employ this principle to our work, even if the tasks we are seeking to complete are relatively humble. Keep going, and we can always get better! Don't use failure as an excuse to procrastinate and instead use it as a motivational tool to make improvements. It is an essential method to becoming more productive and efficient.

Start the Day by Doing the Most Complicated Task First.

Some people refer to this as "Eat the Frog." It relates to starting the day by getting the most unpleasant task out of the way. It is an idea developed by Brian Tracy, who is a motivational expert and first espoused in his book "Eat That Frog."

The theory is that by getting the worst thing over and done with, the rest of the day will seem more straightforward by comparison. It also has the effect of freeing you from worrying about it all day and putting it off to later in the week. Perhaps your most hated task is writing a long, boring expense report for your teams' sales calls? Try doing that first and getting it out of the way.

So, if you want to increase your productivity, you should make a habit of "eating the frog" first thing in the morning. It will make your day more manageable, and you will work more efficiently. Making a habit of all of these methods together will lead to you becoming a more disciplined and productive worker.

Perhaps on the weekend, the most dreaded task is bathing the dog. Start the weekend by ordering Fido into the bathtub! Everything else will be easy.

Get into the Habit of Getting Up Early

There are only so many hours in a day, and the most efficient people around get an advantage by being up and alert before everyone else. Having some alone time in the morning and being able to contemplate and prepare for the day is one of my favorite things. It helps me clear my mind for the day ahead. Many people find that they feel at their most effective in the morning, so I like to take this opportunity to plan my day, work out what needs to be done, and make a start on a few creative ideas.

If we wish to operate at our most productive, most of us will benefit from some exercise so that we can stay in shape and feel mentally alert. Early in the morning is the perfect time to get it done. You can also use this extra time to do something beautiful, which will be mentally rewarding. Perhaps make your kids a lovely packed lunch to take to school (and make a little extra for yourself).

If you are a late riser or are always struggling to get into the office on time, try getting up earlier. You may be surprised that the extra time you have makes you feel more in control and energizes the spirit. It is an effective way of adding to your productivity and is certainly worth adding to your list of changes to make. Start by setting the alarm a bit earlier each day.

The Things we Eat Have an Effect on Our Productivity.

The most productive people around are aware of the importance of eating regularly and using a healthy and balanced diet. A healthy body equals a healthy mind. It is an accepted fact from the World Health Organization that eating the right ingredients can help boost our brain power and concentration.

Maintaining a healthy balance in our diet and trying to incorporate as many superfoods as possible can make the difference between feeling exhausted and feeling like we can conquer the world. I like to eat a big, healthy breakfast to set me up for the day and prepare a nutritious, packed lunch. It helps eliminate the temptation to order a hamburger and fries or a pizza.

Try to eliminate junk food and sugary drinks, which will make you feel like you will crash, and take the time to prepare something healthy and nutritious. If you get into the habit, it is quite quick to do. You should always follow regular meal times and never skip meals. The body likes regularity. Even if you are busy, skipping meals is counter-productive as missing a meal will lower your productivity. So, taking a 15-minute break and enjoying something to eat is a wise investment of your time.

Don't underestimate the benefits of a healthy diet. Making it a part of your day will make you feel better, and it will help your productivity in the long run.

Rewards for Completing a Task are Important

Productive people tend to make a pact with themselves that completing a task deserves something beautiful as a reward. It is an effective method to become more productive. Psychologically, this can be important, and it will encourage us to keep on going when things get boring or tough. Getting through the tough times is vital if we wish to work at our jobs well, so everything helps.

It is possible to train the brain to become more efficient through teaching it. A reward upon completing a task will subconsciously make us want to get onto and achieve the next job and help us maintain a positive outlook. I have a sweet tooth, so something as simple as keeping a jar of sweet candy on my desk works for me. I reward myself with some whenever I complete a project.

Celebrating as a group with your workmates as a reward for completing a task is also an effective way of becoming more productive and has the bonus of helping team spirit. It is an essential method that productive people use, and you should add it to your day. The reward could be anything, a chocolate bar, or a few drinks after work, whatever motivates you.

Exercise is Important

Did you ever hear the expression, "a healthy body equals a healthy mind"? Taking the time to exercise regularly is something most highly productive people practice. A small investment for a gym membership or an even cheaper jogging habit can work wonders for your productivity.

I like swimming, and going to a health club on the way to work to do my laps makes me feel invigorated and alert for the day. It certainly makes me fitter and helps me stay in good shape. Whatever method of exercise you choose, it should be something you enjoy, and it is crucial it doesn't feel like a chore. You can ask the family to join you so you have another activity to do together.

There is scientific evidence of the benefits of exercise on the mind. It can help with your memory and increase your attention span. All of these are essential factors in making you more productive. Just 30 minutes per day of cardiovascular exercise per day can make a tremendous difference in your life and overall health, so those of us aiming to be more productive should add this to our lives.

Planning the Night Before is Key

Highly productive people understand that

worrying is counterproductive. It is far better to plan everything and then get a good night's rest. Poor planning can lead to a stressful day ahead and can give you a feeling of losing control and that chaos is taking over.

It would be best if you considered taking a few minutes before you sleep to plan your next day. It can make all the difference in making your next day a productive one. I like to focus on what I need to get done the next morning and write it down. Even if I have a hectic day ahead, I feel this helps me not to worry and sleep well. I like to wake up in the morning feeling in control of my day ahead and knowing what tasks I will do when I start my workday.

Pre-planning is a vital part of working efficiently and becoming more productive. I recommend that you add this method to your schedule. I am sure that you will notice a difference in your work day.

Learn to Delegate

The most highly productive people realize that it is impossible to do everything. Working hard is certainly a trait that is necessary to become successful, but learning to delegate is equally essential. Even if you have the mindset that success must come at all costs, we are all limited by the number of hours we can work in a week until our productivity starts to drop.

A 35 or 40 hour standard work week is acceptable for most non-disabled workers, but those who push themselves to work much longer hours to achieve success. To become efficient, we need to be able to judge when it is time to delegate. There is likely someone on your team somewhere who is more suited to the task.

I mostly write books for a living, and when I feel inspired, I can write for many hours, but if I go on for too long I lose focus, and I have to spend too much time rewriting because my standard starts to go down. In my case, I find it hard to critique my work, so I write what I think is right and then delegate my work to an editor to review what I have written. It helps to share the workload and ensure quality control.

Whatever your work or business is, you should realize that nobody can do everything and you should seek ways to delegate some parts of your work. Collaboration is a positive thing that allows a different person to give another perspective. We all have different approaches, and we always find ways to learn from each other. If you delegate smartly, you can focus on the overall job and demonstrate the confidence that you have in your team and improves their skill levels. It helps to build a pleasant atmosphere and spirit.

Learning to delegate is an important skill to use if you aspire to be more productive and build an efficient team. Consider what changes you can practically make.

Take Advantage of Technology

It was not all that long ago that we were using a typewriter for reports and a log book for the accounts. The productive people amongst us learn to adapt and take advantage of the latest technology. There are so many apps available these days, which can help us become more productive, that it is vital to take advantage of them. Make a habit of reading about the latest ones.

Some of the best available are Dropbox, Productive Habit Tracker, Trello, and Hours Time Tracking. However, whatever business you are involved in, you will find something of use. As a writer, I was amazed when I first found an app called Grammarly. It can check all of my punctuation and grammar, and even improve the flow and readability of what I write. It has been a Godsend.

We would be foolish if we didn't take advantage of these apps to make our lives easier and more productive. They are there to make our lives easier. It would be best if you investigated which apps will be most helpful to you and start building up what you use. It will give you a boost in productivity and an advantage over your less tech-savvy competitors.

The genuinely productive people amongst us are always looking to get an edge over everyone, and one right way is being knowledgeable about and successfully utilizing technology.

Sometimes You Need to Say "No."

It is human nature to try and do everything ourselves, but similarly to delegating, we need to learn when to say no sometimes. The highly productive person realizes that we are incapable of doing everything, and we need to concentrate on our strong points and what is most important.

When I first started as a writer, it was my instinct to say yes to every job which came along, with the attitude that I would get it done somehow. That is just not a smart approach to working. If you take on too much work, the quality will suffer, so we need to find a polite way to say "no" and focus on the job at hand. One of the most effective ways to say no is to encourage the person who brings the work to you to complete it. You may well be able to advise and guide them to do a good job.

Your time is limited, and learning to say "no" is an important skill to be used if you wish to become more productive. Be selective in what work you take on, and you will see the benefits.

You Need to Set Clearly Defined Goals to Achieve

Truly productive people need to have a clear vision of what they are trying to achieve. You will need to set goals for what you wish to accomplish and within what time frame. You need to avoid being "busy" if you have not clearly defined what you are trying to do.

When I start writing a book, I decide on how many sections and then chapters I wish my writing to contain and then set a realistic timetable. It gives me a goal. Perhaps it is a rough draft of one chapter per day or similar, but the point is I have a goal to achieve and if I do that, I judge the day to he been successful.

Every step you take should be a step closer toward achieving your goal. If you can keep sight of this, you will be taking a giant step toward becoming more productive. It is an important point, so focus on setting proper goals and follow what you decide. It is an effective way for you to increase your efficiency.

Your Work Surroundings are Important

Different work environments work for different people. We all thrive in a space that we feel most comfortable. Think about what it is that you like about your surroundings. The highly productive individual will recognize the value of being comfortable in their work surroundings and the effect it has on productivity.

For some, it can be a conventional office, their bedroom, or even the park. The author J. K. Rowling famously wrote the first Harry Potter book in her local coffee shop. Wherever you feel comfortable is a good place to work. If you prefer to work from home, experience has taught me, you should set a designated work area where you can concentrate and lock yourself away from everyday life.

It is essential to realize that, if you feel comfortable and happy, your productivity and efficiency is likely to increase. Make a point of finding the work location which is best for you.

You Need to Know All of the Shortcuts

Whether you are at home or work, there is no shame in using shortcuts to get the task at hand completed as soon as possible. Most highly productive people practice this. Your time is precious, so if you can get a task completed quicker without compromising the quality, why not do it? Use any useful shortcuts which are available.

An example of this is that in my job, I often need to do much research, so unless it is something of vital importance, I speed read. I can get the essential information in a fraction of the time. I used an app called Spritz Reader to learn speed reading, which has proven to be useful and saves me much time. Deciding to use it has been a wise investment in time and money. Taking the easy route is the smart thing to do in many instances. You should consider which shortcuts you can benefit from and use them!

Learn to Use Automation

It is another useful practice used by highly productive people and can be used in many instances to save much time and be more efficient. It can be a simple message sent by auto-reply to an incoming email informing a client that you will be out of the office for a while or something much more complicated like auto-replies for sales.

Automation is beneficial if you are going on holiday, but can be used regularly and save your business a lot of time and money. I often use automation to handle my email marketing. My business is extremely competitive, and it is vital to answer client inquiries quickly. There are times that I am busy writing, so it is not always possible to handle that myself. So, I found a compelling alternative way. There are remarkably effective programs available now which can answer with high accuracy, often with greater clarity than if I do it myself.

Similarly, I often automate my social media posts. It is a Godsend for me and saves me so much time. There seem to be endless new possibilities with automation. I recently looked at a cloud-based help desk, which appears to be promising. The automated services offered will keep growing, and I am genuinely interested to see what is next. Automated invoicing and lead building apps are now possible, and I am excited to explore that further.

I recommend you look into which facets of your

business you can automate. You will be pleased that you did and will be impressed by how much your productivity will increase. Often, the highly productive people we are discussing are that way for a reason. Their methods work! Let's strive to learn what we can from them!

You Need to Identify Tasks Which are Not Important.

You need to be able to decide what you should give priority. What you choose not to do is an essential part of not being productive. It is a vital skill that you need to learn in the battle to become more efficient. What can you ignore or leave for a later date? Perhaps some administration makes no difference?

There is no point in doing something just out of habit. What is the point? Don't be afraid to change things that waste time. We can all find ways to improve our efficiency. I used to meet with my editor every Monday, which entailed traveling through traffic. Canceling it and communicating via more email made little difference but allowed me more time to be productive.

Recognizing non-essential parts of your work day and eliminating them is an effective way of increasing efficiency and becoming more productive. Analyze what is unimportant in your workday and set a plan for eliminating it. You will save more time than you expect; and time is money.

Music Can be Important.

Highly productive people make good use of music in the workplace. It can be an effective way to improve your mood or just background noise to help you get through a tedious task. I love listening to quiet classical music when I write. It calms my mind, and I believe it helps me focus and be more productive and get more things done.

However, one of my least favorite things to do is typing up invoices. I find this dull compared to writing, so I might well be playing the Clash or the Sex Pistols or something else aggressive to help me get through it. Whatever you think might be useful is worth a try. As you are listening through a headset, you can't bother anyone, and there is no way for them to criticize your taste in music!

There are also some ambient sound apps which can help you concentrate if you are in a loud environment. Search for the latest apps available. Sound can be so crucial in our lives. I went through a terrible period of not being able to sleep properly. Something was bothering my subconscious. I found downloading and listening to white noise while I went to sleep solved the problem for me.

I believe music is an underrated tool in our quest to become more efficient. I recommend you experiment with what types of music will work for you. It certainly helps me to focus and get more done. Anything which helps us with productivity should be looked at seriously.

You Need to Know When to Rest Your Eyes and to Take a Break

New ways of working means that many of us spend extended periods staring at a screen, and eye strain is a real issue to cause concern. When I started as a writer, I usually used a notebook to write, but these days I often spend up to 12 hours in front of my computer. I don't think the human mind can efficiently deal with that.

It is an excellent practice to take a little 5 or 10-minute break every hour. Just take a short walk to stretch your legs or make yourself a hot drink.

If we don't do this, it is too easy to get mentally fatigued and can lead to headaches or other ailments. The mind needs to have a regular break to relax and focus on something different.

Similarly, you need to know when to do something different for a while. Many highly productive people seem like superheroes sometimes with how hard they work, but even they take a break. Going to the park for some fresh air or taking a quick nap under your desk is a great way to feel refreshed and be able to operate at optimum productivity again.

Take the time to take a break from time to time.

Working non-stop is counterproductive and will lead to cloudy headedness and a lack of efficiency.

Having a Tidy Desk is Important

We should adopt the slogan, "tidy desk, tidy mind." It has some basis. How can we work if we are in chaos? Try new methods of avoiding clutter by getting as much done online as possible. Do you need a paper copy for the expense reports? If you do have a job that demands you use lots of papers, take a vow to improve your filing system and keep to it. It will make a tremendous difference in how you feel, and hence, the quality of your work.

An organized filing cabinet within easy reach of your desk may seem an obvious thing to have, but it is far too easy to overlook. Some of us seem destined to be surrounded by clutter. If you do accumulate clutter during the day, ensure that you clear and clean your desk every evening before you finish work for the day.

Try writing a note to yourself saying that this needs to be done before you finish work and leave it in an easy to see location. Making cleaning up each day a regular habit will allow you to start the next day with a clear mind. Productive people work best in an orderly environment.

You Need to Love Your Job

The last method I will recommend to you is to

find something to do that you enjoy. It will improve your life in every way. If you genuinely love your job or business, it is so much easier to be productive. A happy state of mind will always help you to be at your best. All of the advice I have given you so far is unlikely to be useful if you are unhappy in what you do. It is time to do something about it!

Motivating yourself to be productive is so important as the alternative is lethargy, and it is so much harder to do if you are only working on getting by or for the money you make doing it. If you find yourself hating what you do, it is time to reflect on the best way to look at the changes you should make.

Can you make changes in your current job? Perhaps a chat with your boss or a work colleague about changing your responsibilities could help? Possibly being transferred to a different department or finally demanding a promotion would make a difference? If you feel none of these would make you happy, you really should consider a career change.

There are some brilliant adult education programs available these days, and it is certainly possible to combine night classes with a full-time job. I used to run a swimming pool supply business, which was a good business financially. But eventually, I became stale and hated going into the office in the morning. So, I had an honest look at my work life and decided to make some changes. In my case, writing had always been a passion.

I decided to enroll in some writing classes and started taking on some small jobs. It was the best thing I ever did! Now, I feel so much happier and have a degree of flexibility in my life that seemed impossible before. I am indeed a far more productive person since I decided to make that change. I encourage you to look at other options if you are unhappy with what you do. Follow your passion and love what you do for a job. It will make a tremendous difference in how you feel. Life is short, so why waste it in something you don't enjoy doing?

Most truly productive people do what they love. Whether it is running your own business, writing, playing a sport, or designing something - find what you love. We have looked at various practices of highly productive people. They all have their merits. I would like you to consider all of these methods to become more productive and decide which will help you the most.

If you implement these practices, I am certain that you will see an increase in your productivity. Give it a try.

Chapter 6

The Secret Habits and Ninja Mind Hacks to Become the Most Organized Person You Know

In this next section, I will reveal some secret ways to form life-changing habits, which will help you become super organized. There will also be some useful "Ninja Mind Hacks" discussed.

A Few Ninja Mind Hacks to Consider

There is one particular Ninja Mind Hack, which I believe works well, which is always to establish the end of your day. No matter how much work you have to do on each particular day, always have a definitive ending to it. This will enable your mind to focus and be alert to the fact that there is a limited period to get what you need to do completed.

It will enable you to get more done in the limited time that you have as your subconscious mind will be aware of the limits placed upon it and strive to get the maximum possible done. A definitive ending to your day will also help you stop procrastinating and ensure that you will not overwork, which is the enemy of being productive.

Another useful mind hack is to give yourself a reason to work efficiently. It could be more time to hang out with your pals, or teaching your son to ride a bike, whatever works for you. The theory is the reason you give yourself will encourage you to work more efficiently, and therefore increase productivity. It will give you a new reason to work and will mean you don't work harder only so you can do more work. There is also a reward.

There is also a Ninja Mind Hack for people who have an issue with getting started. I used to suffer from this. I could quickly identify what I needed to do and why, but I would take plenty of time to get started without ever really knowing why. Perhaps it was because the whole project seemed overwhelming, and I knew it would take a long time to complete?

The method I used to overcome this was the Pomodoro Technique, which is similar to the idea of egg timers. The theory goes that you set yourself a time limit of 25 minutes to complete a task and then take a break. In this way, an enormous task will separate into small parts which seem much more comfortable to complete than a whole big project. Psychologically, you will find it much more possible to tackle a small project than the whole thing. After completing four Pomodoros, you will have achieved a lot, and it will be time to reward yourself with a more extended break.

It is far easier to get ready to do less than a half hour's work than for a full day's work. I found this an excellent method to overcome my issue with procrastinating. Just take the decision to do one Pomodoro, and at least you have made a start, then the rest will feel more manageable. Over time you will learn to predict how many Pomodoros a given job will take.

Some people are happier concentrating for a longer time and taking a more extended break. So experiment until you find the optimal work and break the pattern. The critical point is to use the Pomodoro method to break procrastination and make a start to your project.

A similar Ninja Mind Hack is the 30 - 30 method. It is when you do intense bursts of hard work for 30 minutes, and then you reward yourself with 30 minutes of doing something fun. It may be a viable alternative to Pomodoros for some people. The reward could be anything: surfing the internet, going to McDonald's, or going to the park - whatever is sufficient to motivate you. Once again, you can experiment with the time periods until you discover which is most suitable for you.

It would be best if you kept a journal of all of the things you accomplish per day. It will have the effect of giving you a sense of satisfaction and pride for what you have achieved. If you start your next work day by looking at this journal, you will feel motivated to achieve more. Subconsciously, you will wish to compete with yourself and do better than you did the previous day. It can be a powerful motivational tool for your mind.

Another thing to try is to have a change in your work location from time to time. It could be whatever you like. For me, I have always loved staying in hotels, even cheap ones. I love the feeling that I can order anything or get an issue sorted out with a quick phone call to staff who are a few meters away. So, from time to time, I like to check into a hotel and work from there for a few days. The change of environment does me some good, and I always get plenty of work done. When I go back to my natural environment, I feel refreshed and happy to be back, which, again, boosts my productivity.

Being unconventional can work as another Ninja Mind Hack. It can work as a way of making you feel as if you are different and can lead to you feeling motivated. It could be doing your household chores when everyone else is out partying or grocery shopping in the middle of the night. Whatever appeals to your sense of being unconventional.

Blocking Blue Light on your various devices is another useful Ninja Hack. Many of us have developed such an obsession with our devices that we can't do without them, even at night time. Studies have shown that extended contact with blue light from our devices can have a severe effect on our sleep cycle.

It is to be avoided at all costs (as we have discussed earlier), because a good night's sleep and feeling rested are one of the main factors in being at our most productive. Most up to date devices have an app to block blue light, but in case they don't you can download something practical. Whatever you do, don't let something so simple as exposure to blue light lead to unproductivity.

A straightforward Hack which you may not have thought of is to turn off all notifications of your devices. With no Twitter, Facebook, or email updates, you will be free to focus on the task at hand. You can assign a set period per day to deal with those notifications and use the rest of the time to get more things done.

A recent trend in Ninja Mind Hacks is intermittent fasting. It is an exciting idea which people believe makes our minds more focused and sharper after fasting for 12 hours. The theory is that at the point, our bodies naturally start using our stores of glucose, which has the effect of producing ketones, which are useful for encouraging brain metabolism. It could well be that new Ninja Hacks for our bodies could be the key to achieving higher productivity. It is an area which is worthy of further study and experimentation.

Consider using a "mind dump." It can be useful when you start to feel stale and frustrated with the job you are working on completing. Just write! Whatever comes into your mind, without worrying about grammar, spelling, or structure. Just let whatever is on your brain out. Let it go! You may feel refreshed after (even if what you wrote is nonsense!) and feel more able to get down to doing some proper work.

We all get stir crazy sitting in our offices sometimes. If you start to feel that you can't get anything done and are being unproductive, go outside. Break the pattern by doing something different for a while. Go for a walk, a hamburger, or even a beer. Just find a way to break the cycle. When you get back to the office, things will be different.

A short change of scenery and just letting the mind think about something else for a while is often the cure for when you feel that things are not getting done. Just be sure to tell someone where you are going, so that you don't experience the same thing I once did. Some emergency happened when I slipped out for an hour, and I was the only one able to deal with it. I returned to panic and chaos as nobody had any idea where I was!

The final Ninja Mind Hack I will recommend is Time Stretching and Attention Training. The basic concept is to have a period each day where you allow your body to go into a time of intense focus on something other than work. It would be meditation, competing in sport, playing an instrument, or working on an artistic project or some similar endeavor. The focus and effort you put into this practice will make you more perceptive and have a generally positive effect on your health.

All of these Ninja Mind Hacks will be beneficial in increasing your productivity and enable you to work smarter. You should add as many as possible to your day to day practices as is possible.

Secret Habits to Declutter and Get Peace of Mind Quickly

As we have discussed elsewhere, decluttering is a step-by-step process which can take a lot of time. However, peace of mind is helped by decluttering and it is an essential part of being productive.

In the following section, we will look at some quick methods we can use to achieve peace of mind in a matter of minutes. All of these are effective ways to improve your state of mind - quickly!

- It would be best if you went through the pile of old mail that you have been accumulating for months.

- Quickly go through your house, collecting all old mail, flyers, and other useless papers. After checking there is nothing essential - junk the lot!

- Everyone has a drawer somewhere which is full of junk. It is time to tackle it! Take it out and turn it upside down.

- Only put back things which are useful and serve a purpose. Junk the rest!

- Do a laundry run and then neatly sort it out and put it away.
- Many of us regularly feel the laundry building up and threatening to take over the house. It is time to get it done!
- Once it is all clean and put away, a weight will lift from your shoulders. Make a promise to yourself, never to let it build up again.

- Look through your bathroom and throw out everything that you don't need.
- The bathroom is another area where we collect unnecessary clutter. Old newspapers, magazines, shampoo bottles, and others are redundant. Why are you keeping them?
- Another room has had a decluttering makeover in a matter of minutes.

- Look through your closet and throw out your old clothes.
- Most of us have a closet full of clothes we haven't worn for years. It is time to get decisive and junk or send to the charity shop what we don't need as a part of the renewal process we are undertaking.

- Clean out your refrigerator and throw out everything that you won't use.

➢ Firstly, remove everything inside and then give the refrigerator a good clean. Only put back things which you are sure you will use.

There is a load of clutter to dump using this method, and the best bit is it won't take long! Small steps matter in the overall process of becoming more organized. Doing quick decluttering in this way, and promising yourself not to let clutter build up again, is an essential step to becoming the most organized person in your group.

Every unnecessary item we own will work on our mind in some way. Taking these quick and straightforward steps is the right way of clearing your mind as well as your home.

Most of these things only take a matter of minutes, so why not do them today? Psychologically, you will feel better and ready to become more productive.

Organize Your Household Papers

We have all been in the situation where we are desperately searching through a pile of old papers looking for something important. What do we do when we can't find a bill due today?

It is time to get organized and sort out the household documents as part of the decluttering process and becoming more organized. You may be amazed at how many documents you find stuffed into drawers or closets, or just sitting on counters or tabletops.

Here is a proven method to get this issue sorted out, and once it is, we should make a pact with ourselves not to let it happen again. Promise yourself, write it down, and follow your promise!

- Round up all of your documents and put them all into one pile.

- It will allow you to go through them and separate the important ones from the junk. Be brutal and throw out anything which is not essential. There is no room to hoard junk!

- It would be best if you took advantage of finally doing this job to set up a proper filing system for anything important.

- Have a look through your documents to see what you can digitize.

- It is time to get more high-tech with your simple household documents. Most smartphones or tablets can download a scanner app which will allow you to make digital copies which are easy to store.

- Aside from any legal documents, everything else should have a digital copy made and then discarded. It means more clutter is permanently gone!

➢ Make it a habit to scan, save, and discard any new non-legal related household documents you receive.

- For any essential documents, you need to have copies made.

➢ For anything important like land titles, birth or marriage certificates, wills, and the like, it is essential that you make a backup copy and put the originals in a safety deposit box or similar at another location.

➢ If you were to lose these documents due to flood or fire, it would be time-consuming and expensive. For your safety and convenience, this is a critical step to take.

- Buy yourself a filing cabinet and set up a proper filing system.

➢ You will be amazed by how much stress having a proper filing system will save you.

➢ Buy a proper filing cabinet and other supplies such as files, labels, and others. You can then divide everything into categories such as bills, receipts, warranties, personal documents.

- If you do not have too much in the way of relevant documentation, you may be able to get by with a large folder. As long as they are all filed away, you are making proper progress!

- Try to reduce the amount of paper you use in the future.

- After you have scanned and saved as much as you can, you should investigate other ways to cut down on paper.

- See if you can sign up for digital versions of household bills, bank statements, and others. These are all far easier to archive and store online than if you are collecting more unnecessary paper.

- Over some time, you can put into place a system which will enable you to do a significant amount of decluttering and take steps toward getting organized.

- Taking control of your household documents and finally getting them sorted out is an integral part of becoming more organized, both mentally and practically.

It may seem like a small step, but it is a significant one. There is no reason not to start today. Being more organized is an essential step to becoming the most productive person in your group!

Make Sure You Keep Up your New Habits

Which Have Allowed You to Become Organized.

All of these methods of improving your organization are not much good if you cannot maintain these new habits. If you fall back into your old ways every time, there seems little point in trying to become more organized.

I will share a few tips on how to retain your new good habits.

- It would be best if you started with something simple and not try to change too much at once.
- ➢ Find a simple first change to make and stick to it. Turn it into a habit. An example here may be to get into the habit of digitizing all of your household documents.
- ➢ If you try to make too many changes at one time, you will likely not stick with them long term and not form positive organizational habits.

- You should celebrate (in a small way) if you succeed.
- ➢ If after say three months, you have been able to keep up your good habit of decluttering, you should reward yourself.
- ➢ Becoming more organized is something to celebrate, even if the habit you have picked up is something small.

- Realize that you won't always get it right and mistakes are possible.

➢ To err is human, so don't get too down on yourself if you break some of your excellent new habits.

➢ If you slip up - don't give up! There is something worthy about having a decluttered house or a clean work area.

➢ Whatever it is, please pick up and start again without letting things get as bad as they were before. Get organized once again and double down on your determination to follow good habits and be disciplined.

Adopting these steps I have suggested into your routine is an excellent way to develop positive new habits and a critical step toward becoming a more organized individual.

Don't Make These Mistakes When You Try to Become More Organized.

The goal of becoming more organized and trying to declutter your life to become more productive is a worthy one. However, there are a few critical steps to avoid.

- Don't invest in new storage before you start.

- ➤ You may think that buying storage boxes, cabinets, files, and other items before you start is a good idea, but it is not.

- ➤ Do the clearing up and decluttering first and then calculate what you will need for storage.

- ➤ If you get the wrong storage things in advance, you will have a beautiful collection of new clutter, which defeats the whole point of what you are doing.

- Don't be too ambitious and take on too much.

- ➤ Decluttering and organizing your home is a big job and will take time to achieve. Do it in an ordered manner so that you don't lose motivation.

- ➤ A few hours of work which does not start to feel tortuous is better than doing a whole day and ending up hating it and giving up.

- ➤ Small but smart steps are best. Just aim to do what is realistic. You likely can't do your whole house and office in one day. Take your time and plan for it to be a long term project.

- ➤ You should feel good about what you have achieved, even if it is just a small step. It should keep you motivated to keep going until everything is complete.

The Productivity & Decluttering Master Plan

- Make sure you complete the task.

  ➢ You will likely have a lot to do to complete decluttering your whole house. Be realistic and set a time frame to achieve this.

  ➢ Decide what you will do with the things you will throw out. Surely, there will be much garbage, but separate the useful items that you no longer need. Some could go to charity shops or friends.

  ➢ One crucial step is that once your decluttering is complete, you need to complete the task by disposing of everything.

  ➢ There is no point separating everything into separate piles or bags and leaving it there. It defeats the purpose of what you are doing.

  ➢ At the end, take the time to throw the garbage, drop by the charity shop or deliver something useful to a friend.

  ➢ Finally, the clutter is gone, and disposing of it will have its mental rewards. It is an achievement!

- Don't fall into the trap of thinking this is a one-off job.

  ➢ Decluttering and becoming more organized is a long-term task. You will need to repeat this unpleasant process many times, but hopefully not on such a large scale.

- ➢ You need to be determined to be disciplined and not let the unnecessary clutter build up again. You are now an organized person!

- ➢ Your organized new home will look great, and you will feel a sense of having accomplished something by decluttering, but make sure you are prepared to do it again.

- ➢ If you want to be the most organized person in your group, this needs to be a permanent change.

- ➢ It can take over two months for a new habit to become second nature. So, expect to be doing plenty of more clearing up during that time.

- Don't expect perfection.

- ➢ Things will inevitably build up again from time to time. We spend a large part of our lives in our homes, so it is natural that we may collect unnecessary junk.

- ➢ Don't be disheartened when it happens. We are human, and after all, we aim to become the most organized person in our group - not to become perfect!

These secret habits and Ninja Life Hacks that I have shared with you are an excellent way for you to become a more efficient and productive person. You need to be disciplined and do it. If you can implement the majority of these into your day-to-day life, I have little doubt you will be by far the most organized person in your group of family and friends.

Chapter 7

How to Manage Your Daily Actions to Become More Productive and Achieve More

There are many ways in which we can more effectively manage our-day-to day actions, which will lead to is becoming more productive and achieving more. In the following section, I will discuss various ways for us to achieve that.

Firstly, I would like to discuss in greater depth the fantastic opportunities provided by technology to increase productivity. In my opinion, the invention of the internet and the accessibility to new and up-to-date information it has provided us has been very valuable. The web is the single most significant advancement we have made in history.

How to Easily Organize and Declutter Your Technology

Getting rid of e-junk is a constant battle for most of us. The popularity of cleaning apps for our phones and tablets is a testament to that. There are several favorite apps which perform this function.

Some of the more well-known include Phoneclean, CleanMyPhone, and Tenorshare for iPhone and Clean Master, DU Speed Booster and CCleaner for Android.

These are simple examples of ways in which we can declutter the devices which have become such an essential part of our everyday lives. The unnecessary accessories and data stored on our devices can be comparable to the inessential data that we store, which prevents us from working at our optimal level of efficiency and productivity.

There is certainly a popular trend for many people to declutter their lives and homes. Downsizing and throwing out unnecessary possessions is becoming popular. There is plenty of unseen data in our technology, which we should also consider purging. There is a vast amount of digital junk from old work reports, long-forgotten screenshots, and photographs which haven't been looked at in many years which we can afford to lose from our devices.

There is also plenty of hardware cluttering up our houses. We must all have multiple old phones and laptops hanging around unused. Our homes have wires, headsets, and cables which have lain unused and forgotten for ages. Why do we hold onto such pointless junk? The instinct is probably to think that it "might come in handy for something one day."

I am a gadget freak. I spend practically all of my spare money on yet another smartphone, tablet, or some accessories. I think I am uniquely qualified to comment on collecting junk. The question is, what we should do about it?

In my opinion, the biggest culprit is the various power cables we accumulate for each different gadget. For example, all of my laptops smartphones, cameras each require a different type of wire, which is annoying. My penchant for collecting the latest interesting gadget means my collection of cables grows by the month. The best way to handle this is to have a tech decluttering session. Gather your whole collection of cables and be decisive.

Brutal action is required, and you should throw out everything except what you use. Nobody is ever going to need the Nokia 3310 charger which has been in a drawer for ten years! If you don't know what it is used for, it is safe to say that you can throw it out without too many worries. Accessories such as these are so cheap to order online these days that anything you have accidentally thrown out you can easily replace.

Similarly, with old cell phones or tablets, if you have not used them for an extended period of time, it might be time to donate them to a charity shop. In our attempt to become technologically organized, we need to stop the disorganized spread out over the whole house. It is time to choose a drawer for everything tech-related to living!

Digital hoarding should be our next target. The data that we leave behind on our gadgets takes up valuable space and makes searching a more complicated process. We need to be disciplined and every once in a while spend a little time losing the junk on our laptops, phones, and tablets. It is not complicated and is quick to do. I recommend doing this at the end of each month, which will make the battle against e-junk more bearable.

Photos are a massive user of our limited data, purely because most people take so many. Many people never delete anything and think of it all as a fond memory. Perhaps we should be more particular in what we keep. Is the pic of the great hamburger we had five years ago necessary to keep?

This decluttering process is just as crucial to our mental process as it is to regain some space on our phones. We are carrying around our clutter with is on our phones. Addressing all of this is a normal part of managing our daily lives. If we can solve the clutter in our heads in a similar manner, we will make progress towards becoming highly productive.

Make Good Daily Use of Up to Date Apps to Become More Efficient

There are so many useful apps being rolled out on a seemingly daily basis that it is time to incorporate the best of them into our everyday business practices to aid with productivity. It is time to stop just using apps for fun and contacting friends and choose helpful apps to help our work rather than as a distraction. The time is now to use our devices for good!

There are just too many to review in an overall manner so I would like to take a look at a few apps which I believe to be particularly useful. It is worth spending some time going through your chosen Android or iOS store to check what is available and applicable to your business regularly.

Some of the apps I recommend you investigate further are:

- 1Password
  - 1Password is a useful app which can save us time by storing all of our passwords in one place. It is 100 percent secure and will assist you in selecting strong, hard to hack passwords.

- Grammarly Premium
  - Grammarly Premium is an excellent app if you work in a business where it is vital to get grammar, structure, and spelling 100% correct.
  - It will save you a tremendous amount of time, as it acts as a lightning-fast proofreader and will make suggestions about how to make

improvements. For a relatively low investment, your work life will be more comfortable.

- ➢ It is like a super powerful version of autocorrect. There is also a free version which is useful for testing the app or if you only need it for very light use.

- Google Drive
- ➢ Google Drive is an excellent app, especially for those that need instant access to files, especially when working on the road.
- ➢ Instant access to all of your company's files and documents from anywhere with an internet connection is a dream that would have been unimaginable for most people ten years ago.
- ➢ There are free options and a very reasonably priced version for hefty business users.

- Google Docs
- ➢ Google Docs is an excellent free program which is ideal for writing any documentation. You can log on using any Android or Windows device through your Gmail account.
- ➢ I use this app all of the time, and I find the smooth interaction with other Google apps such as Gmail and Google saves me much time and helps with my productivity.

- Hours Time Tracking

> Hours Time Tracking is a useful iPhone app which helps with keeping track of the time, scheduling, and using a virtual calendar.

> An added advantage is that it is a free app which integrates well with an Apple watch.

- OmniFocus

> OmniFocus is another Apple app, which is like a genius version of a to-do list. It is available in free and reasonably-priced versions depending on your needs.

> The big difference here is that it is a smart app that can set reminders depending on your location or with whom you are interacting. It certainly is a way to improve efficiency and boost productivity.

- Paper

> Paper is an Apple app which allows you to convey your ideas to work colleagues efficiently. You can sketch drawings, write diagrams, or make handwritten notes to show or send to others.

> It is excellent for sketches as it utilizes a touch screen and is so easy to draw or create on. It is a

unique way to speed up the creative process and quickly share your ideas with others.

- Click up

➢ This app is available on both Google Play and Apple. It is an effective way to combine your to-do list with the agenda of your team.

➢ It enables you to see the status of projects, the next projects which need to be done, and comment on the state of other colleagues' work.

➢ You can easily share ideas, notes, or files and it is one of the better productivity apps that I have used. I recommend you install this free app now!

- Discord

➢ Discord is a cheaper, but equally enjoyable alternative to the popular Slack app. It is used as a communication tool and is particularly useful for collaboration on a project with remote colleagues.

➢ Team chat is a simple process as there is voice communication for multiple users, and the most expensive option only runs at $4.99/month.

➢ If you require an effective and economical communication tool, you should seriously consider Discord.

- Be Focused Pro - Focus Timer

  ➢ Earlier on, we have discussed the need to be focused and clear our minds to concentrate on a task to be truly productive. This Apple app is an effective way to help us to achieve that.

  ➢ This app blocks distracting apps while you work on a task and allows you to set specific tasks which need to finish within a particular time.

  ➢ One great feature is that you can specify break times so you can set productive work intervals. You can also set work targets for a whole day.

  ➢ It is a competent app to help with work targets, especially for those of us who work well with work then a break. It is also customizable to schedule meetings into your workday.

- 24me

  ➢ This app works as a personal assistant to sync all of your calendars together. These could include, Yahoo, Microsoft 365, Google, and whatever else you may use.

  ➢ It gives you greater control over all of your work and personal tasks and makes scheduling a far more straightforward process. It is available for free on both the Apple and Android platforms.

- Dropbox

> Dropbox is a popular app which is available on both Apple and Android platforms, which allows for secure document storage and sharing.

> It allows you to organize and comment on files in a straightforward way. It is excellent for mobile devices, and you can check complex documents on your phone while you travel.

> It is also easy for your team to stay in touch and make comments on each other's work. It is an excellent tool to increase teamwork and productivity.

- Evernote

> Evernote is an Android and Apple app, which has the tagline "Meet your second brain."

> It does indeed feel like that when you start using it. Most of us have millions of creative ideas running through our minds, which all too often get lost and forgotten.

> It is a great way to save ideas on whichever device you have to hand, however random they may be.

> This app is available in free, basic, and premium versions and is worth checking out for the most creative thinkers amongst us.

- FocusList

- ➢ We discussed the Pomodoro technique at length in a different section, and this app is ideal for helping you follow that.

- ➢ The basic idea is to use the technique for time management by using 25 minutes of intensive work, followed by a 5 minute break to be at our most productive.

- ➢ This app helps us to plan this time management, and it also allows us to review how effectively we've worked at the end of the day.

- ➢ It is one of the most effective and easy to use Pomodoro timers available on the market.

- Forest

- ➢ Forest is another free app which is available on both Android and Apple platforms. It is a time management app which focuses on blocking distractions.

- ➢ It has a fun concept which turns discouraging you from picking up your phone into a game.

- ➢ You are given a seed to grow a tree and you are rewarded with your tree growing if you leave your phone alone while you are supposed to be working.

- ➢ Your tree will wither and die if you pick up your phone too often.

- You can compete with your family and friends. Surely nobody will want to be the bad guy who lets a tree die?
- The concept is a good one, which, in a fun way, will encourage you to leave your phone alone while you should be working and, thus, help you be more productive and achieve more.

- Lumen Trails
- This app is a free Apple productivity tracker. It allows you to track things such as calories consumed, what you do, what you spend, and how much sleep you are getting.
- Usually, you would use a separate app for all of those, but this brings all of those functions together into one app.
- It gives you feedback on your habits through quick notes and helps you identify problematic issues and encourages you to focus on increasing productivity.

- Pocket
- Pocket is a dual free Apple and Android app which helps you to bookmark and store new articles to come back to later.
- It is particularly useful if you are researching a project and are finding interesting information

which you do not have time to read thoroughly at that moment.

➢ You can come back to it later, and it will be presented on an easy-to-read interface. You can also grade how essential or interesting each article is so that the app will rank items for you.

➢ They also offer you a reading list which will be suitable for your interests.

- Productive Habit Tracker

➢ Productive Habit Tracker is a free Apple app which encourages us to follow habits which we hope to do every day.

➢ You can add habits you wish to follow, such as writing in your journal, taking Fido for a walk, going to the gym, meditating, or writing a daily report.

➢ Whatever you wish to get done, the Productive Habit Tracker will send you reminders and encourage you to get them done.

Whether you have a preference for Apple or Android, there is a vast range of useful apps available which will help you improve your efficiency and productivity. It is a current reality that you need to take advantage of these and boost your efficiency. Your competition is most likely using something similar, so don't allow your opposition to gain an advantage in productivity.

Vow to Take Better Advantage of e-Commerce

I have been hugely impressed with the fantastic developments with e-commerce. There seems to be no limit to what is now available online. If, for a moment, we consider online shopping, we can now order practically anything we can find in the shops, often at a much lower price. Delivery is quick, and modern technology means there will not be any mistakes. When we consider how time-consuming traditional shopping is, it seems productive to shop via e-commerce.

The old doubts about using credit cards online, and fear of using your real identity for online transactions are mainly in the past, so there is an excellent opportunity for us to save time by shopping online. We would be foolish not to use the time saved to do something more productive. After all, there is always plenty of more work to do.

E-Commerce, more generally, has opened up so many opportunities in other areas. There is often no longer a need to send bills and send someone to collect the money. Why? It can all online. People can establish whole businesses, selling a wide range of stock without ever renting a building, or holding even 1 dollar worth of stock. There are options for the automatic answering of client inquiries, collection of leads, and automated billing, which will completely change the way we do business.

The future for e-commerce seems unlimited, and anyone who wishes to be more productive would be foolish not to stay fully informed of the innovations and learn to take advantage of them. It is a remarkably useful tool for increasing productivity and efficiency; and the influence of e-commerce will only spread in the future. Making e-commerce a day-to-day part of running our businesses will undoubtedly lead to us operating more efficiently and productively.

As we have looked at, there are various options to help us manage our daily operations and become more productive. We need to find the best combination of these methods for the business we are involved with, and they will surely help us to work more efficiently and achieve more.

Chapter 8

How to Triple Your Productivity Overnight With One Simple Strategy

It may seem impossible to triple your productivity in a short time, but the fact is that it is possible. Being more productive is mostly a state of mind, and there are many ways to achieve his state. There is one particular strategy which I have found most effective, and it has allowed many people I have taught it to to be able to increase productivity dramatically overnight and me.

It is mindfulness. The idea is that you are consciously aware of what you need to do and actively consider what you can do about it. If you concentrate on improving your state of mind and your intention to be productive, things will improve. It would be best if you decided to be more productive.

Mindfulness has become increasingly popular in recent times. Indeed it can now be described as being fashionable. It can be described focusing all of your awareness on what is happening at this moment. It enables us to focus on the present, the "now," if you will, and be aware of precisely what we are trying to achieve.

This may seem like such a simple thing, but when we are mindful and focused on our thoughts, we realize that we spend far too much time considering the past and the future. We are all too prone to daydreaming about trivial matters rather than focusing on the task at hand. How we deal with this is key to becoming more productive.

We need to find a balance. Many of us naturally spend too much time having our thoughts focused on the future, the past, or the present. It is not productive to spend too much time in the past or the future, or to focus so strictly to the present that we fail to learn the lessons of history, so we need to seek balance.

When we use mindfulness effectively, it allows us to be thoughtful of what is on our mind and the present time. It is a habit that we are well-advised to adopt as we have a likelihood of focusing too much on what we will be doing next week, next month, or next year. Using mindfulness will stop our brains' wandering and allow us to focus on the now and become more focused and productive.

What are the Benefits of Mindfulness

Having better focus is one of the main benefits of being mindful. Our minds being distracted is one of the most significant challenges to becoming more productive. While we are trying to focus on the job at hand, our brains tend to lead us to think about the hundreds of other things we need to do. We may feel obliged to check our email or walk out and talk to the sales team, just due to a nagging feeling that there is something to be done there. We may then jump to thinking about needing to take our child to soccer practice later and that our partner expects a nice dinner tonight.

Frankly speaking, our brains are always looking for a distraction and are prone to wander. Mindfulness is one way to improve focus and increase productivity. It is the best way we have to bring ours mind to order and get focused on the now and allow us to finish the task at hand. Mindfulness also allows us to practice better planning. These two things complement each other perfectly. If we plan, we can focus less on what we are concerned about and this will allow us to practice mindfulness more effectively.

A proper plan and a schedule for everyday duties are straightforward if we apply mindfulness. It can enable us to find an appropriate place for what we need to do day-to-day and leave time for focusing.

Reducing stress is a significant thing that mindfulness can help us achieve. Too much stress is caused by thinking about the possible negative consequences of our actions. If we can focus on the job at hand, we will not suffer stress due to this. Unfortunately, our brains are wired to speculate on the future, so it is hard to overcome stressing about this. Therefore, we need to find methods to manage this issue. There is no benefit to stressing over possible future issues which haven't happened yet. It is a ridiculous habit.

Mindfulness can help us realize this and bring our stressful negative thoughts of the future back to the present and understand the future should not be having an effect on the now. This use of mindfulness can be beneficial in dealing with insomnia caused by worrying about the future.

In my younger days, I suffered greatly from insomnia. It turned me into a physical wreck. Sleep deprivation is not helpful if you write for a living. I had been through years of misery with insomnia when a friend helped me realize that it was fear of what may potentially happen in the future, which was causing it. Mindfulness was what helped me overcome it. It made me realize there is nothing to fear.

We need to replace the negative thoughts about bills that we will pay and bosses that need to be made happy with more comforting ideas. Mindfulness can help us consider that things are not so bad. The bed is warm and our family is okay, our boss appreciates us and nothing too awful is about to happen.

You can use this moment to reflect that the future is not yet here, the past is past, and overall, the present is pretty good. Learn to appreciate and live in the now.

Fear and Mindfulness

Fear will change with mindfulness. You may believe that fear in various forms is stopping you from being more productive and effective. Anxiety can be the enemy. If we could choose between being fearful and fearless in our personal lives, most of us would choose the latter.

Many of us suffer from a lack of clarity about our decisions and reluctance to make risky choices due to fear. We should not have to feel restricted by this. We should not feel regret for being withheld from making bold choices due to an irrational fear of what might happen. Fear is a frightening feeling which often stops us from reaching our full potential. No matter how much we may try to avoid it, fear is something we all feel to some degree.

I used to suffer from many fears throughout my life, mainly when it came to my career. I worried I was not a good enough writer, I worried I might not make it, and I feared I might be broke. I stopped thinking about this and decided there was only one way to find out - work and see. I realized I needed to conquer my fear, and looked at various ways to find a way to overcome it.

Mindfulness is the solution. Realizing that fear will be overcome, the future is not yet here, and it probably will not be anything to fear at all. We also need to understand why we fear the unknown. A step into darkness always seems scary due to us not knowing what to expect. If what is in front of us is unknown, it will always be challenging to take the next step forward.

It is a very human reaction to be wary of what will happen next. We are predisposed to prepare ourselves mentally and physically for what may be around the corner. Emotions are a complicated thing, and they play a huge role in overcoming your fear of the future. Be mindful and base your feelings on reality, not an irrational fear.

Another consideration is how to increase your level of confidence. You need to understand yourself and your limitations before you can tackle your fears. It would be best if you aimed to be the best possible version of yourself, and an excellent way to achieve this is to boost your self-esteem and become more confident. It will help you overcome negative fears.

If you suffer from low self-esteem, the challenges presented to you in everyday life can seem insurmountable. Anything from making a speech in class to dating can become a traumatic experience. Low self-esteem can lead to a negative view of the world and even lead you to develop a "victim mentality." The world can seem a difficult place to conquer if you reach this state. It can lead to you feeling worse and your self-esteem falling further; and your productivity will suffer.

A boost in self-esteem is a crucial way to boost your productivity. If you suffer from low self-esteem, you will never be at your most productive. Fortunately, whatever level your self-esteem is at, there are various ways to boost your self-confidence. You will feel better overall, and your productivity levels will improve. In many cases, low self-esteem starts with how you perceive yourself and how you think you should be.

It can start in childhood with a thoughtless comment from a relative. The offhand comment saying you did something stupid or that you are fat can have long term consequences. The way that others treat or see you has a considerable effect on your self-esteem. However, the solution to this comes does not come from external factors; it must come from within yourself.

Improving your self-esteem is not easy to achieve; however, with the right methods and support, it is possible. There is a hidden power which can lead to a fantastic boost in productivity, if we can resolve our self-esteem issues. Some strategies to try include:

- Find out what is the real problem you have. There can be many triggers, and the use of therapists or simple mindful thinking can lead you to a greater understanding.

- Always do your best. It is a simple, but essential step. If you feel you are doing your best every day, you will feel pride in yourself.

  ➤ If you are disappointed by an outcome to a project, ask yourself if you did your best. If you did, there is little else you could have done. You should feel satisfied.

- Try to see what others see in you. Positively do this by imagining how the one who loves you most sees you.

➤ In my case, it would be my grandmother. If I see myself through her eyes, it is easier to see myself in a positive light.

- Do things that you enjoy. They are essential to give you a feeling of well-being and satisfaction.

➤ When you enjoy what you are doing, whether it is hanging out with friends or a hobby, it makes everything seem worthwhile, including yourself!

- Accept the good and evil within yourself. Whatever has happened to you throughout your life, appreciate yourself.

➤ Bad experiences always teach us things and make us stronger. Appreciate that you're well-intentioned and always do your best.

- Be aware of who you are and be proud of that. Identifying your real self and accepting it as a fact will lead to you improving your self-esteem.

➤ You don't always need to "fit in" with the in-crowd. Learn to appreciate your good points, and accept your weaker ones, more.

- Compromise less and be stronger. Everyone wants to appear friendly but putting everyone else's needs before your own is not the way.

➤ It will have negative consequences for you. It is necessary to realize that your needs are essential also.

- Always aim to look for the good in yourself. If your self-esteem is low, you will likely only see the negatives when you look at yourself. It has to change.

➤ You have probably gotten into the habit of seeing your worst side. Be mindful of your good points and concentrate your thoughts on those. Your self-esteem will improve.

- Stop thinking of yourself negatively. Don't worry about the mistakes you have made. They are in the past.

➤ If you tell yourself you always screw up and make mistakes, you will believe it. It's far better to say to yourself that you are capable and incredible as you will think it also.

- Value and appreciate your relationships. As our self-esteem is reliant on how others see us, make sure you surround yourself with positive and nurturing people.

➢ Appreciate people who know and love the real you. They will enforce a positive self-view by recognizing your better attributes.

- Take risks. A big part of being successful is experiencing failure. It will help you build resilience, character, and self-esteem.

➢ When you overcome failure and achieve something, you are getting stronger. At the end of your days, don't regret not taking enough risks.

- Always have a goal in life. No matter how modest it may be, it is essential to always have an aim as each time you achieve it, your self-esteem will improve.

➢ It is too easy to allow the fear of the unknown to stop you from achieving what you should in life.

If you follow these steps, they will go a long way toward improving your self-esteem and allow you to increase your productivity levels. One of the best things we can do to overcome fear is to understand our purpose in life. It will help us understand the unknown and conquer our fears.

Our sense of purpose can boost our productivity as it will increase the way we feel. A spiritual and emotional feeling of well-being can stimulate the mind to achieve more. Sometimes finding the meaning of our lives means more than happiness. Happiness is an emotion which can come and go; being mindful of our purpose can be a more effective way to be productive. The meaning to our lives will encourage us to be at our best during the good times and keep struggling through during the tough times. The meaning and purpose of life can help overcome fears as it allows us to know what our aims are and where we intend to end up.

Visualizing the future is your friend. It is a compelling method to rid yourself of fear. It is a way of rehearsing the future, to be better prepared for what you may face. Studies have revealed that visualizing what may happen has a similar effect on the brain as real action, so in a way, you are training your mind to be healthy and unafraid.

This practice can help you stay motivated, improve self-esteem, and put you on the way to achieving maximum productivity. It is another example of the power of mindfulness and allows us another way to improve our effectiveness. If you consider all of these points and act on them to use mindfulness, you can triple your productivity overnight.

The improved focus, overcoming your fears, better planning, and determining to be less affected by stress and its side effects are all critical components to becoming a more productive and happier individual. It is possible to become more productive in a short space of time. You should start practicing mindfulness today!

Chapter 9

The 3 Scientifically Proven Things You Need to Stop Doing Right Now in Order to Get More Done

We can all agree that we typically need to find a way to perform better and get more done. The trick is to find the most effective way. We will next consider the three scientifically proven things we need to stop doing right now in order to get more done.

The things we stop doing can be more important to our productivity than the things we are doing. We spend far too much time working on negative things and finding ways to eliminate them is vital to improving overall productivity. The medical community has been proving that attitude can have an effect on our health for the past 50-plus years. There are countless studies showing how harmful negative thinking can be.

The three scientifically proven things we need to stop doing right now in order to get more done are:

- We need to get rid of negativity in our lives.

- We need to stop constantly looking at our social media sites.

- We should pay more attention to our ultradian rhythms.

We will now consider these three scientifically proven points in turn in our effort to understand how we can be at our most productive.

How to get rid of Negativity in our Lives

Negativity is the enemy of productivity. We need to get out of the habit of saying "I can't," and become more positive and optimistic. The fact is, you "can" do anything, and if you don't know how yet, you can learn!

If you have a bad habit you wish to break, such as spending hours reading online when you should be working or an addiction to smoking, don't say "I can't" but find a way to make sure you "can."

A negative mindset will ensure that you fail. It is a trap that too many of us fall for. The way you think means the difference between success and failure. If you find yourself doubting your ability to do something, keep telling yourself "I can do this, and I will do this". If you truly want to improve your productivity, changing the way you approach every day challenges is an important way forward.

Having some negativity is a human way to be and is easy to understand, but having too much will just make you underachieve and make life harder. A pessimistic attitude will make everything seem negative and make it impossible to achieve the success we want. Make a vow to adopt a more positive attitude and enjoy your new positivity. You need to be proud of your strengths and view any weaknesses as just something you are working on improving.

Boosting your productivity will mean stopping negative habits. This may seem hard to do, but start now and you will see that after just a few weeks, your productivity will be improved. There are various ways you can try to reduce negativity in your lives and these are proven methods to try:

- Body language is important. It has more meaning to our mindset than you may realize. If you are slouching or frowning, you are more likely to be thinking negatively.

  If your body language is poor it can affect how people see you and this can have an effect on your self-confidence which in turn leads to negative thinking. Focus on improving this. Sit up straight, smile and be more confident when you deal with other people.

  You will start to feel better if you improve your body language, and this will help you lose your negativity; improved productivity will follow.

- Change the way you think. Sometimes changing your perspective of the things around you can help. Instead of thinking of everything as a, instead think of it as a challenge.

  There is a huge difference between thinking, "I will never finish this sales report by tonight," and "This is a challenge and it will be a real achievement to get done on time". The two are very similar, but the positivity in the second statement will allow you to banish negative thoughts and make a huge difference to your productivity.

- Some things need to be discussed to solve issues and get pent up emotions out. Keeping things to yourself can build up your frustration and lead to negative thought patterns. If there is something you have been holding onto which should be discussed, you should take the opportunity to discuss it with someone.

  A simple discussion and hearing another person's opinion can help you put things into perspective. This can help you realize that the issue at hand is not so bad, and you can solve it. This will help you overcome a negative attitude toward it.

- Take a short time-out to calm your mind. We all experience a cluttered mind from time to time and confusion leading to a racing mind. It can be hard to maintain control over your thoughts and stop negativity creeping in.

Just take a minute to calm things down. Some people like to meditate, I prefer to have some candy and stare out of the window. Empty your thoughts and restart your task; you will find much of the negative thoughts have gone.

- Go for a walk. If you are stuck with a negative mindset, you're better doing something to change it. As negative thoughts occur in the mind, it is easy to conclude that is where they come from, but there are other factors.

We can't always choose who we work with, and negative people can cause you to follow a similar thought process. Sometimes the best choice is to take a break from this atmosphere. Head to the park, people watch, or have a drink; just do something to change the negative vibe.

This will improve your state of mind and you will be more productive when you return to work. The short time off will be more than made up by your improved mindset.

- Do something creative. Embracing your creative side is an excellent idea to overcome negativity. Find a creative outlet, whether it is writing, painting, or building something. It will lessen your negative feeling. Creating is always a positive step.

This can act as a form of therapy as you can release your emotions through a creative process. It will help you reduce negativity and become more productive.

- Take time to notice the good things in life. It is too easy to forget the things we should be grateful for. It could be the nice lifestyle your job allows you or the love of your family, but most of us have plenty of things to be grateful for. When we get stressed by day-to-day life, we stop focusing on the things that are going well in our career and family life.

    Just because your boss shouted at you or you had an argument with your partner doesn't mean it is all bad. Accentuate the positive. Physically making a list of all that you should be grateful for is a good start. It helps us focus our mind on the good things in life. This will stop us taking things for granted and failing to see the good things. We will forget negativity if we focus on the good. This is a powerful tactic to use in overcoming negativity and is certainly something you should try.

- Laugh at yourself. It is too easy to take things too seriously when life gets busy, so you should practice seeing the funny side. We all have our foibles and strange ways of doing things - we should laugh at them. If you don't take yourself too seriously, you won't get trapped into negativity.

Learning to laugh at our mistakes and silly behavior will help us realize things are not so bad; and make us feel happy. Our happiness will lead us to positivity.

- We should strive to help others. Negativity and selfishness are related, and in order to find a purpose to our lives we need to consider others. If we can find our purpose, we will become more positive. It is the simplest way to become more productive.

You can begin in a small way; be polite, hold a door open, or inquire how a colleague is doing. All of these will give you a sense of worth that will be helpful for positivity.

- Form your own team of positive people. There is no better way to overcome negativity than to spend time with a group of positive people.

In the same way that negative thinkers lead us to negativity, the positive people in our lives encourage us towards positivity. You should put your own support team of positive thinkers together. They can be relatives, friends, colleagues from work, or whatever; as long as they are positive people. You should aim to meet with them regularly, for a drink or a lunch, and feed off of their positive vibes.

This will have a great psychological effect on you and help you fight off feelings of negativity until you next meet up.

- Become more aware of your surroundings. Start to pay attention to the small things and appreciate the day-to-day things we deal with. Learn to appreciate the beauty of nature more, laugh at things more, spend time hanging out with your pet more. You should note how you feel doing all of this. This awareness of the interesting and beautiful that surround us is an excellent way to decrease negative thoughts.

- Learn to identify what makes you unsatisfied. Sometimes it is hard for us to identify what it is we want in life. An effective approach to this is to consider what we don't want. Most of us have something that we don't like in our lives. Perhaps it is a lack of skill or knowledge or a negative person who you know you need to lose.

  Consider these points for a brief time and then focus on how different your life will be if you finally do something about it. You can use what you don't want to identify what you do. Positive changes will have a dramatic effect on your mindset. You will feel better and become more productive.

- Find out what motivates you. It could be increasing your prosperity or providing for your family; perhaps something as simple as an extra holiday per year. These thoughts will give you an aim in life and something to strive for. Test sense of achievement you will feel while building for your aims is extremely rewarding.

It will lead to positive thoughts and a "can do" attitude and when you achieve your aims, your sense of well-being will be boosted. It will help you to reduce your negativity and focus on what is possible if you try.

- Accept that you are still learning. It is easy to get trapped, in our career or our relationship, by a feeling that we can't improve our situation. If you can accept that we are not all-knowledgeable and are still learning, there is always hope that things will get better.

Take the chance to do some more studying, read a book, or even consult with a therapist. The learning process will help you understand your situation better. The extra knowledge which you acquire will help you know there is a better future and this will help you have a positive attitude. Knowledge is a powerful way to overcome negativity.

- Take a moment to realize how strong you really are capable of being. We all face challenges in life and it takes a great deal of internal strength to face up to them. We are all vulnerable to feeling sorry for ourselves, but when we consider our lives, we should recognize what an incredibly resilient machine we are every day.

Take pride that you can overcome difficulty so well. Focus on the fact that every hardship has made you stronger. This will allow you to improve your self-esteem and acknowledge your strong points. Human beings have an awesome power.

- Learn to enjoy your work day. Instead of viewing your job as a chore which has to be done, focus on the good things that it brings you. Even if you find your job boring and not much of a challenge, it does bring good things to your life. Think of what your salary gives you the freedom to do and the pleasure that you get from a chat with a friendly work colleague.

  One of the challenges I initially faced as a writer, was the lack of day-to-day interaction with work colleagues, so I consciously made friends in my field of work. Making the best of it and enjoying what you do is an important way to encourage positivity.

- You should take some each day to let your imagination wander. Turn off your appliances and consider your dreams and fantasies. It is a great mental process to let your mind run free, and I find I get some of my most creative ideas when doing this process. Your dreams and fantasies are something unique to you and will help in your quest to have a positive mindset.

- It is a good idea to consider how long your goals might take. We have discussed how having goals leads to a positive mindset. It is worth considering how long they might take. Short term goals help us feel good about ourselves when we achieve them. Something that will take many years to achieve might cause you to lose interest, so it is helpful to consider what is possible in the shorter term.

   For example, you may have always wanted to learn a musical instrument. This is perfectly achievable in a relatively short time. The pleasure this will give you and the sense of pride you will feel when you achieve this will have a great effect on your mindset.

- You should always reevaluate your goals and find new ones. It is important to keep moving forward with what you wish to achieve. Nobody likes the feeling of stagnation; it leads to boredom and increases negative thought patterns.

   You can set a time every month to consider how much progress you have made towards your goals and what you can do to improve your progress. There are always new goals to be set, and you should aim to add a few more every month. I try to set a goal to learn a new skill every month, even if it is something simple. As I am a writer, I aim to learn five new words every day.

These seemingly small steps help me overcome negativity, as having something to aim for focuses our mind on the positive.

- We should realize that our relationship habits have an effect on how positive or negative we feel. There are certain things such as being married, owning a pet, laughing, and having a loving relationship, which are scientifically proven to make us happier. These things can also have a drastically positive effect on our health.

  There has been plenty of research which shows the link between heart disease and not having strong links to family and friends. Loneliness can seriously impact our health and state of mind, so we should be conscious of this and consider what we can do to improve our personal relationships. If we have a positive relationship with family and friends, it will be difficult to get caught up in negative thought patterns.

  A nice side effect to this is many studies have shown that this can increase your lifespan. A long and healthy life can be attained with positive relationships and habits.

- You should learn to forgive and forget. One of the most beneficial things we can do to decrease negativity is to forgive. If we forgive others, we can get out of the pattern of negative thought. It is one of the most healing things we can do for ourselves.

There is no point in holding onto old vendettas and worrying about arguments from long ago. You should just let it go. Life is too short to have hatred in your heart for something that doesn't matter much in the great scheme of things. Forgive and forget. Does the stupid bit of gossip someone said about you really matter that much?

Try this method. Forgive someone today. You will see that you will feel better. You will get rid of negativity and will become more productive.

It is scientifically proven that if you can stop being negative, your productivity will improve. Please take on these points I have raised to overcome negativity. If you implement what we have discussed, I am confident that you will be well on your way to creating a positive mindset that will make you a powerhouse of productivity.

Once your thoughts become more positive, you will feel happier and be better equipped to deal with the challenges that life sends you. It is beneficial if you can find the right balance in your life. Don't spend too much time working and give plenty of time to your family and friends. If you have strong relationships, your mindset will be stronger and positive things will start to happen.

When you become a happier and brighter person, life will seem easier and better opportunities and the opportunity for greater prosperity will come your way. It is time to stop struggling with negative thoughts and embrace the thought that human beings have a tremendous capacity to create a wonderful life. We all have tremendous opportunities in our lives and it is our duty to find a way to take advantage of them. Negativity will only work to stop us reaching our full potential.

We need to surround ourselves with as much positivity as possible, whether it is thoughts, upbeat people, good deeds or forgiveness. If we wish to be as productive as we can possibly be, we need to learn the lessons which we have discussed and act on them!

The new positive and productive you is well within reach. I advise you to start making changes in your life to achieve this today.

We Need to Stop Constantly Looking at Our Social Media Sites

The incredible rise in the influence the internet has had on our lives over the past few decades has had both positive and negative influences. Of course, the access to information and entertainment has led to us being better-informed and given us better access to quality entertainment.

I am a fan of boxing and I find it unbelievable that I can watch practically any fight worldwide live on my iPad. It was not that long ago that I would have to wait months to find out the results. So while there are clear benefits, we do need to consider the downside also. Addiction to social media is a real problem for many people. There is now such a wide range of choices of social media such as Facebook, Twitter, Instagram and Snapchat, that we are almost overwhelmed by choices to use.

There is a temptation to use all of them and this will have a devastating impact on our productivity at work. Even if we are not using it, we are thinking about it when we see something interesting. Even in our home lives, many of us find ourselves doing less, even spending less quality time with our families. There are millions of people worldwide who keep their social media accounts live 24/7. Is this really a healthy way to live?

It was not so long ago that we only used phones for talking to people. The long term effects of this are still unknown, but we have certainly undergone a drastic change in the last decade. While a lot of important things do happen, it is a fact that many of us waste a huge amount of time every day with frivolous things on social media. We should focus on limiting our access to social media, especially when we are trying to do some work. There is always too much temptation to randomly get chatting to a friend or watch another cat video.

It is a good idea to limit your social media use to one or two designated sessions per day, otherwise you will get distracted and your productivity will suffer.

We spend too much time interacting with people online, and we need to maintain real life relationships in order to properly bond with people and feel properly supported. While it is true to say that many businesses use social media in a positive way to promote their services or products, it does come with some risk.

The obvious risk is to do with time management. If an employee is tasked with using the company's Facebook account, the temptation to waste time by using their own accounts will always be present. It can take some time to refocus on the job at hand if you have started to look at some great pictures of your summer holiday location. It also disconnects the employee from interacting with others in the office and having a good work relationship.

There are many mental health professionals who fear that short attention spans and an inability to concentrate will be a side effect of prolonged social media use.

There is also concern about the effect social media use has on overall mental health. Many intensive users have reported that they suffer from high levels of stress. There needs to be a long term study as to the effect social media has on our mental health.

The mental health of your employees can impact directly how your business performs. You need content and motivated employees to be productive and have great relationships with others. A stressed employee can have various physical and mental issues which will affect their ability to have effective communication with clients and work to maximum capacity.

Social media can also be a source of misinformation. Fake news has become a popular expression and it is a fact that misleading online content can damage your business. Social media can also blow small things out of proportion. All companies or employees make errors from time to time, and if you have an incident go viral it can be a public relations nightmare.

There is also the Fear of Missing Out (FOMO) phenomenon, which entails a fear that you may be missing out on a fun or interesting experience that someone else mentions on social media. It is a form of anxiety which is fueled whenever you use social media and the more you use it the more likely you are to see someone else having fun you might not be having which adds to your stress.

Another side effect of spending too much time on social media is the negative effect it can have on how you sleep. I freely admit that I am a Twitter addict and I have to check it if I am awake for any reason. Even a trip to the bathroom in the middle of the night can mean going back online for an hour or more. It will eventually lead to sleep deprivation and this will certainly impact on our ability to work effectively and lower our productivity.

Cyberbullying is often thought of as an issue that young people face, but it is still a factor for adults even within a company. It comes in several forms such as nasty emails, fake photographs, gossip, and threatening private messages. Employees who have experienced cyberbullying often report extremely high stress levels which can affect their ability to perform in an effective manner.

There is also a potential for tension amongst colleagues who follow each other's private pages on social media. Jealousy can be a factor as can controversial opinions about politics or sports. Unfortunately, in the world we live in, opinions can divide us and cause problems. It can be a danger to harmonious relationships in the workplace, which can have an effect on team spirit and productivity.

So we can clearly see that there are negative side effects to using social media and limiting use of it is essential in the modern workplace. If you are experiencing any of the more severe symptoms, such as stress or depression, it might be time to consider giving up on social media altogether.

We Should Pay More Attention to Our Ultradian Rhythm

We all experience a drop in our productivity after focusing on a task for an extended period of an hour and a half to two hours. This is a scientifically proven natural occurrence which is known as the Ultradian Rhythm. It is something that we need to stop ignoring. When you feel mental fatigue, you need to ignore the temptation to keep on going and "push through" the lull in energy you are feeling.

You would be far better off taking a short break and having a cup of coffee or a snack, or better yet a quick sleep, before going back to work with a more focused attitude with more energy and creativity.

Your body will use this time to refocus, recover, repair and rebalance. You will feel refreshed and capable of your next burst of activity.

A fifteen to twenty minute break can make the difference between an efficient day and a day of sloppy work. It can guard against stress and fatigue. What you definitely do not want to do is keep doing what you have spent the past few hours doing, which is probably staring at a screen.

You need to perform a "human reboot" by changing scenery for a while and concentrating on other things. Other activities you could try are; taking a bathroom break, going for a quick walk, looking at the sky, meditating or doing some deep breathing, yoga, letting your mind wander, or paying a visit to a friend.

In fact, any change of scenery and doing something different will be beneficial and make you feel better when you do get back to work. If we reach the state of feeling distracted and groggy, our immunity drops, our mental capacity is comprised, our metabolism goes haywire, and we will be irritable and moody.

In fact, we get less productive and the more of these breaks that we miss, and the more we risk damaging ourselves. The more you learn about Ultradian Rhythm, the better you will understand your own needs and be capable of improving your productivity and focus. This seems like such a simple thing to consider, but paying attention to your Ultradian Rhythm is one of the best things you can do to improve your productivity.

These three scientifically proven things which we need to stop doing are all effective in helping us get the boost in productivity that we are seeking. Experience has told me that each of these three steps will enable you to feel better about yourself and allow you to achieve the maximum efficiently that you can.

Chapter 10

Conclusions We Can Draw About Improving Productivity and Decluttering our Lives

I do hope you have enjoyed listening to my theories about how we can declutter our lives and seek better productivity in our work and personal lives. If you practice the techniques I have shown you, it will have a positive effect on your life and improve your situation at work and home.

A lot of the things we have discussed are common sense, and you are likely to use them to some degree already. There is no harm in thinking more deeply about ways we can implement these productivity methods to a more effective degree. I recommend you spend a part of each day reflecting on what we have discussed and decide which of these ways of improving your productivity are most suitable for you.

As we have discussed, there is a lot to consider when we seek to declutter and improve our productivity. We have looked at various methods to improve our productivity, which has covered effective processes to improve our attitude and state of mind. Decluttering in all parts of our lives is a positive step to improving overall productivity, but it is not at all easy to achieve.

It takes a long term determination to change our habits and thought processes. It seems the human brain is wired to go back to old negative patterns. To increase our productivity, decluttering is an important step to undertake. It should not daunt you as we have been through various methods to help you achieve this.

Decluttering is more than a physical process and can have tremendous mental benefits also. The discipline involved can help reduce negativity and put us in a positive frame of mind. We can all agree that we have room for improvement in our lives, and finding the best way to declutter is a significant step toward becoming a more productive person.

We know that modern life is increasingly about competition. Improving our productivity is the best way to gain an edge in our competitors and achieve the success we aspire to have. We have discussed the most effective methods to utilize the power of positive thinking and work to improve our mindset to be as effective as we can be.

There is no single way for any of us to reach maximum efficiency, and we now have the information to make incremental changes and work on different methods to have an overall effect. There are many ways to gain control over a given situation.

Mastering this is a crucial element to being at our best. If we are stressed or worrying about minor issues, we are likely to overreact, be ineffective, and achieve less.

Finding a good work/life balance is vital to enjoying our lives and getting into a good frame of mind. Negativity is the enemy of productivity. As we have seen, there are ways to change the pattern of negative thinking. If you conquer your negative thought processes, you will have a happier and simpler life and be a long way towards being at your most productive.

To have a successful life, we don't just need to consider what we achieve work-wise; we need to ensure our family is happy and what we can do to help society as a whole. These methods to improve your productivity and declutter your life have come from a lifetime of experience, and I hope you get the desired effect when you put them into practice.

I wish you positivity, a decluttered life, improved productivity, stable home life, and above all else, prosperity and happiness.

***

www.ingramcontent.com/pod-product-compliance
Lightning Source LLC
Chambersburg PA
CBHW070944080526
44587CB00015B/2218